ARE YOU READY?

Jim Sheppard —
A career announcing Illinois
football and basketball

BY FRED KRONER

Published by
The News-Gazette, Inc.

The News-Gazette®

EDITOR AND PUBLISHER   John Foreman
PROJECT EDITOR   Amy Eckert
EXECUTIVE EDITOR   John Beck
MANAGING EDITOR   Dan Corkery
SPORTS EDITOR   Jim Rossow
PHOTO EDITOR   Darrell Hoemann

Mike Goebel
Fred Kroner
Joan Millis
Walter Pierce
Amy F. Reiter
Jim Sheppard

Front cover photo: Jim Sheppard by John Dixon, The News-Gazette
Cover design and book layout: Joan Millis, The News-Gazette

Soft cover ISBN: 978-0-9798420-0-9

Printed in the United States of America

The News-Gazette, Inc.
15 Main Street
Champaign, IL 61820
Phone: (217) 351-5252
Fax: (217) 351-5245
www.news-gazette.com

DEDICATIONS

To my darling cousin, Tena Sprau, who was more like the sister I never had.

— FRED KRONER

To my mother, Lucille Kirby, for her unconditional love and support; to my wife, Joan, for her quiet strength and for being the beautiful person she is; and to my grandsons, Caden, Camrin and Charlie. You three little ones are the joy of my life and may you enjoy reading about your "Papa" when you are older. I love you all.

And, to Fighting Illini fans everywhere!

— JIM SHEPPARD

IN MEMORIAM

Naomi Kroner, mother

— FRED KRONER

Mary Jane Mines, sister
Lyle Sheppard, father
Don Kirby, stepfather
Charles Wikoff, father-in-law

— JIM SHEPPARD

ACKNOWLEDGMENTS

*No book would ever be as good as it turns out without the efforts of
the eagle-eyed editors. Two of the best reviewed this manuscript.*
Amy F. Reiter, a News-Gazette reporter, provided the first read and caught
such mistakes as a reference to Jim Sheppard as a "pubic address announcer."
And Mike Goebel, a News-Gazette sports copy editor, provided the final read
to make certain the finished product read smoothly and was grammatically correct.
Special thanks to Cindy Edman, from the Utah Jazz's media relations office, for her
efforts in getting comments from Dee Brown during the heart of the NBA playoffs,
and to Cassie Arner and Derrick Burson, from the University of Illinois sports
information department, for helping track down current UI athletes.
Joan Millis, News-Gazette art director, took the words and created the
layout and design of the book so that all involved are proud to say
they were associated with it, and, of course, a huge thanks to
News-Gazette publisher John R. Foreman who encouraged the
undertaking of the project and then provided an exemplary introduction.
It is also impossible to overlook Walter Pierce, a circulation sales manager at
The News-Gazette and the go-between for so many sources as well as one of the
marketing coordinators, and Amy Eckert, The News-Gazette's Director of
Community Relations and Special Projects who helped oversee the project.
Last, but not least, a special thanks to my wife, Emily Kroner,
who continues to be the inspiration for all that I do.

— FRED KRONER

My gratitude to The News-Gazette for the creation of this book. Special thanks to
author Fred Kroner, to Amy Eckert and Walter Pierce for their marketing efforts,
to Joan Millis for design and layout, to Mike Goebel for his proofreading and to
News-Gazette Publisher John R. Foreman for the wonderful foreward.

— JIM SHEPPARD

TABLE OF CONTENTS

FOREWORD

It's the atmosphere, as much as the action, that explains the enormous appeal of college athletics.

And for those seeking their entertainment in the big-time sports arenas of the University of Illinois the past two decades, a significant part of that atmosphere — and at least some part of that appeal — has originated with Jim Sheppard.

For 22 years, Sheppard has been "the Voice of the Illini" manning the public address system in Memorial Stadium and the Assembly Hall, one of a very few figures who could bring fans out of their seats without ever walking onto the playing area. He was one of the even fewer better recognized by sound than by sight.

It was Sheppard, after all, who ignited the faithful before each contest with the booming rhetorical query, "ARRRE YOU READY?" And it was Sheppard who forcefully affirmed when you witnessed a "First and 10 for the Illini," or "Deeeeeeeeeeee for Threeeeeeee!"

But there is far more to announcing a game than a sonorous voice or a clever tagline. It's as much science as art, demanding careful preparation, rigorous attention and a sometimes vigorous schedule. Those listening to Sheppard's signature sound over the years came to expect perhaps one part cheerleader and nine parts dispassionate professional. While nearly everyone else in the arena enjoyed the luxury of losing their heads from time to time, Sheppard's job was to maintain the steady, reassuring tone of a true pro — skillfully masking the reality that he bleeds Orange and Blue as readily as anyone who has ever set foot in the arena.

Professionalism was always among the first qualities mentioned when award-winning News-Gazette sports writer Fred Kroner asked athletes and coaches about "Shep." That comes as little surprise to those of us here at the newspaper, where Jim has held a day job as an advertising professional through many of the years he spent evenings and weekends in the press box. This books owes much to several of his newspaper colleagues, including Amy Eckert, Walter Pierce, Joan Millis, Amy F. Reiter and Mike Goebel.

But even those of us who know Jim well can find much that's revealing in Kroner's look at the man behind the voice, the work behind the scenes and the insight behind a long and illustrious career as one of the best in the business behind the microphone for the Fighting Illini.

Are you ready?

John R. Foreman
Publisher
The News-Gazette

CHAPTER 1

For members of the vast and vociferous Illini Nation, one voice means game time.

Season ticket-carrying members of the University of Illinois have heard of Jim Sheppard and, more importantly, they've heard Sheppard.

He is a person who disregarded the adage many of us were taught as tykes: be seen and not heard. He followed the opposite path.

Sheppard's deep voice resonates throughout Memorial Stadium on those autumn Saturday afternoons when the University of Illinois football team is

Jim in first grade.

playing a home game. Yet, few folks see him at his perch high atop Memorial Stadium in the press box.

Neither rain nor snow nor heat nor cold can silence Sheppard. He has been behind the microphone for 135 consecutive UI home football games, a streak that covers 22 straight seasons.

When the shoulder pads and helmets are in storage, Sheppard takes his familiar and comforting voice across the street. In February 2007, he completed his 22nd — and final — season as the public address announcer for home Illinois men's basketball games. He worked more than 340 games.

"The big thing you noticed was the booming voice," said Brian Barnhart, who works for Champaign radio station WDWS and handles play-by-play for Illini football and basketball games for the Illini Sports Radio Network. "His booming voice was a big part of the Assembly Hall and Memorial Stadium experience for a generation of fans."

Barnhart included.

A graduate of Unity High School, located just south of the UI campus in Tolono, Barnhart was a fan years before he started his broadcasting career.

"He was part of what was going on at Illinois," Barnhart said.

Folks might not immediately recognize Sheppard's face, but when it's matched with the voice, he becomes one of the best-known UI personalities.

There is a reason for that, according to Doug Pugh, a stagehand who has done audio at the home basketball games since 1988.

"If you listen to a tape of him from 20 years ago and from yesterday, it's the same," Pugh said. "Jim is one of the most consistent people I've been around. He had a routine, not unlike an actor or a musician."

A native Midwesterner, Sheppard grew up following the Illini and continues to do so. And yet, when it's time for him to take the microphone, he avoids the rah-rah qualities that make some announcers a target for the critics who prefer to hear an impartial person speaking.

Sheppard was, quite simply, one of the best.

"He is as good as any I've been around," said Ron Turner, the Illinois football head coach from 1997 to 2004. "He had a unique style and brought some entertainment to it. He was not blah or mundane.

"He was so good, I didn't have to make any requests."

Turner's successor as the UI football coach, Ron Zook, has learned not to underestimate the importance of the person behind the microphone.

"I think a good P.A. announcer is integral to the overall atmosphere of a game," Zook said. "They can be a direct catalyst for the crowd and their enthusiasm.

"I know the atmosphere during the Final Four (basketball) season was very impressive for someone just joining the Illini family."

As a lifelong UI fan, Sheppard felt a part of the scene long before he was officially hired.

"Because of my long connection with Illinois athletics as a young fan, member of the media and then as the public address announcer, I always felt a special connection," he said. "It becomes part of who you are. There are so many fond memories and special times that I was fortunate to be a part of."

In a 1986 newspaper interview, Sheppard was quoted saying, "I probably get as psyched up for the games as the players and coaches."

He just does so in a different manner.

"When I said that, I was referring to the anticipation factor," Sheppard said. "Obviously, I don't slap the side of my spotters' heads or bump their chests, but the anticipation of the game day atmosphere is certainly there."

Fairness is one of Sheppard's prominent traits, said former Illini basketball head coach Lou Henson.

"He was an outstanding professional," Henson said. "He did the job, and he did a great job. He was ideal for college.

"He was always prepared and very conscientious. If he didn't know how to pronounce a name, he found out beforehand. He did an excellent job for our fans over the years."

Sheppard will start his 23rd season as the P.A. voice of University of Illinois football when the 2007 home season begins Sept. 8 against Western Illinois University.

4

Lou Henson, Illinois basketball coach
from 1975 to 1996.

CHAPTER 2

Some folks are naïve about the responsibilities of the P.A. announcer. It goes beyond the response once given by a clueless non-sports fan when discussing the duties of the man at the microphone.

"Is that the person who tells us if our car lights were left on?" the person wondered.

While Sheppard gives relevant announcements, his primary job is to keep the fans informed about the game. He introduces the starting lineups as well as the coaches, he provides information on statistical leaders at halftime and after the games. He also commemorates milestones.

One such announcement came Jan. 12, 2005, after the Illini basketball team defeated Penn State 90-64. Sheppard told the 16,618 assembled spectators: "Tonight's victory marks yet another milestone in the 100 years of Illinois basketball. Tonight, your Fighting Illini recorded their 1,500th victory in school history. The Illini are proud to be the 11th winningest team in NCAA history. Congratulations, and Go Illini."

Following a pause, Sheppard added his standard closing: "Again, thank you for your attendance and have a safe journey home."

Before the contest starts, he contributes to the excitement surrounding the game without showing disrespect to the visiting school. "Are you ready? ... It's time for Fighting Illini basketball," he would say moments before tipoff.

One former Illini basketball player would routinely acknowledge the comment before Sheppard would ever speak it.

"Right before the starters stepped on the court to start the game, they would wipe the bottom of their shoes in front of the scorer's table," Sheppard said. "Sergio McClain (1998-2001) would always look over at me and lip sync, 'Are you ready?' "

Illinois coach Ron Turner and defensive coach Mike Mallory, right, watch as Justin Harrison (32) runs back an interception against Michigan on Oct. 16, 2004, at Memorial Stadium in Champaign, Ill. The Wolverines won 30-19.

A Peoria Manual graduate, McClain was the only player, Sheppard said, that "I remember being a little loose before tip-off. Once he stepped on the court, it was all business for the Peoria warrior."

Regardless of the rooting preference for fans, the energy generated from the cheering throng created the perfect environment for the beginning of the game.

"There's no doubt that how they approach it, the tone of voice, keeping the excitement going, how they present things, it can all make a difference," current Illinois basketball coach Bruce Weber said.

"I think you find that out as you go around to different schools and different arenas at the college and pro levels. You realize how important the P.A. announcer can be as far as adding to the atmosphere."

When an injury occurs, especially in football where fans are farther from the action, the P.A. announcer lets the spectators know who has been hurt.

And who can forget Sheppard's declaration at football games when the chains are being moved? "First and 10 for the Illini!"

Said Ron Turner: "He had a great first-down call. I remember him pumping the crowd up and getting them going."

Turner's predecessor as Illinois' football head coach sang similar praises.

"I always appreciated what he did at the stadium," said Lou Tepper, who guided the Illini for five seasons, starting in 1992. "There are certainly all kinds of announcers.

"Some are true homers. Some are kind of bland. There are those that are professional and yet they can, through the excitement and enthusiasm in their voice, move a crowd. Jim added to the wonderful environment with his professionalism. I'm glad he was there to work with."

Former Illini Stephen Bardo currently works at ESPN
as a college basketball analyst.

CHAPTER 3

Former Illini basketball player Stephen Bardo said it's important not to underestimate the value of a quality public address announcer. He said Sheppard was able to influence the spectators.

"What he can do is sway a crowd to get into it," said Bardo, now a college basketball analyst for ESPN. "He can be exciting on a particular call, like a dunk, and can have a big-time effect on the overall mood of the crowd."

Despite having that power, Bardo emphasized that Sheppard did not overstep his limits.

"He's calling the game for the Illini, but he understands that people expect professionalism," Bardo said, "and he did that throughout his career."

Bruce Weber said there are different challenges in basketball than football, but added, "I think you can (create excitement) in both sports.

Former Illinois coach Lou Henson, center, does color commentary with one of his former players, Stephen Bardo, left, and Brian Barnhart for the Illini Sports Network during the Illini's 89-64 victory against Southeast Missouri State on Dec. 28, 2005.

Illinois coach Bruce Weber gets after one of his players on Jan. 25, 2005, at the Assembly Hall. The Illini beat Minnesota 77-53.

In basketball, they are more up close and you've got more of an up-and-down flow where things can happen very quickly. There can be more of a lull between plays in football, but they can also react more to big plays and touchdowns because the action stops, so I think they can make an impact in both sports."

Lou Henson said Sheppard's longevity in the business made him "part of the establishment."

Bardo believes Sheppard's presence helped both players and fans feel at ease in their surroundings.

"Jim is almost like part of the institution," Bardo said. "When you go (to the Assembly Hall), there are things you expect to happen, things you grow to love.

"Jim is a voice of consistency, and to hear his voice and to anticipate his calls on plays you know are going to happen is very comforting. It almost feels like home."

Weber agreed.

"When you go to a lot of games, you get accustomed to a voice and connect that voice to a particular school," he said, "like what has happened here with Jim having done the games for so many years."

Weber said he successfully blocks out much of the commentary while focusing on the game, but he's aware of what's being said.

"I'll pick things up here and there," Weber said, "especially the 'Deeeeeeeeeeee for threeeeeee' that caught on, but I notice it more when I'm watching game tape with the volume up. I'll hear things that grab my attention."

Childhood football in Fisher. The bruiser
on the right is Jim at 7 years old in 1955.

CHAPTER 4

Former UI football coach Mike White — the last coach to guide the school to the Rose Bowl game in Pasadena, Calif. (Jan. 2, 1984) — said Stephen Bardo's points are equally valid for the sport that takes place at Memorial Stadium.

Jim and former Illini football coach Mike White, left, at Memorial Stadium.

"He had one of those great voices and can fire up a crowd," White said. "He had a tremendous reputation and was the perfect guy for Illinois sports.

"His enthusiasm and knowledge of sports are

what set him apart. I was always impressed with his accuracy."

White called Sheppard an important Illini contributor.

"He was part of Illinois and part of our success," White said. "We fed off of each other."

There was one reason his tenure is counted in decades and not years.

"Some of those (P.A. announcers) wave the banners for their teams and it's distracting," White said. "He stood the test of time because he made his points at the proper time. You could sense his enthusiasm, but he was very professional."

Scott Nagy had an up-close look at the Illini while attending Champaign Centennial High School in the 1980s. His father, Dick, was an assistant coach during Lou Henson's regime. Scott Nagy is now the head coach at South Dakota State University.

"It seems to me now that the trend with a lot of (P.A.) guys is to be loud and exciting and that puts the attention on them instead of what is going on," Scott Nagy said. "The game should attract the attention, not the announcer.

"For me, hearing Jim brought a level of comfort. It's what I was used to for about 10 years. That's the main thing for most fans, the comfort of having the same person you get used to."

J Leman, a Champaign Central High School graduate who will play his senior season as a linebacker in 2007, appreciates that Sheppard doesn't try to cast himself into the limelight.

"Jim did everything in a tasteful manner," Leman said. "He made the game about the team and not about himself. He didn't try to steal the spotlight from the players.

"I don't know if it is just because I am from Champaign, but I prefer Jim to other announcers that I have heard."

Lon Kruger, an ex-Illini basketball coach who left to coach the NBA

Atlanta Hawks, said it would have been out of character for Sheppard to act differently than he did.

"His delivery was respectful," said Kruger, who now coaches at the University of Nevada-Las Vegas. "He respected the game too much to get too far out of the center. He had a lot of pride in what he did and how he represented himself.

"He's one of the best, without question, and doing it 22 years, it's not surprising he has gotten very good at it. He had such a good feel for the flow and the crowd. He was a real first-class professional."

Brian Barnhart, from WDWS, has seen the trend "in the NBA, where they're going towards more of a production than just an announcer," but he prefers what Sheppard offered.

"He was more in a traditional role," Barnhart said. "He gave you the facts and all the pertinent information, too, and had his own unique

John Dixon/The News-Gazette

Illinois coach Lon Kruger talks with point guard Frank Williams during a break in the action against Northwestern on March 4, 2000. The Illini won 73-44.

style. He had a good sense of when the crowd was excited."

Like a fine wine, Sheppard felt like he improved as he aged.

"The longer you announce, all the details that go into announcing a football or basketball game get smoother each season," he said.

Jim's
sixth-grade
photo.

CHAPTER 5

In the summer of 1985, UI Sports Information Director Tab Bennett was charged with finding a replacement for public address announcer Tom Trent, who moved to California.

Bennett, a Miami native, lettered in football at Illinois from 1970 to '72 as a defensive end and earned All-Big Ten accolades his final two years.

"Tab and I became good friends after his playing days," said Sheppard. Bennett was interested in whether Sheppard wanted the opening.

At that time, Sheppard had returned to Champaign and, he said, "Tab didn't know where to contact me."

The UI SID had to do some detective work.

"Tab called a mutual friend of ours, Connie Vogt, who had worked at WDWS for many years," Sheppard said. "Connie also didn't know where to reach me, but knew that my mother was employed at Tepper's China in Champaign."

Eventually, the word reached Jim that he was wanted and "the rest is history," he said.

When they spoke, Bennett "told me other candidates were being considered," said Sheppard, who didn't audition for the position. "As the summer weeks rolled along, I never heard from Tab if I was still in the running.

"With the 1985 season opener against Southern Cal quickly approaching, I wanted to start my preparation work if indeed I had been chosen, so I called Tab and asked if he'd made a decision."

Bennett, the first African-American SID in the Big Ten, told Sheppard he had the job. Bennett and Sheppard worked closely over the years until an auto accident in Indianapolis during the 1989 NCAA Tournament contributed to Bennett's declining health.

"The last time I saw him was at a Friday night press dinner on campus. When I noticed him at dinner, I was shocked that an illness had taken his once-strong, athletic body down to a little more than 100 pounds. I gave him a hug and we spoke briefly.

"Tab passed away a short time later."

In March of 1994, Bennett died at age 42.

He was succeeded by former assistant Mike Pearson, who had no inclination to change announcers.

"Jim is a very caring guy and I was happy when he took over as the P.A. voice," Pearson said. "There was no hesitation for me at that point to have him remain in that job.

"Whenever there is an administrative change, people in those (supportive) roles have a little apprehension what would happen, but there was never any doubt in my mind that Shep owned that job."

Sheppard, meanwhile, was never asked to sign a contract to become the P.A. personality. He was paid modestly on a game-by-game basis.

"The job was always year-to-year," he said, "although every year, the DIA and I never really discussed the next season."

Sheppard said in his early years with basketball, there was no set dress code.

"I always tried to look as professional as possible because I was representing the University of Illinois and the men's basketball program," Sheppard said. "In later years, the scorer's table crew had to wear Big Ten sweaters and a white shirt.

"The conference prided itself on looking as uniform and professional as possible because more people watch Big Ten basketball games on television than any other league in the country."

In football, there was no dress code.

Sheppard followed a standard routine in preparing for his assignments. He attends the weekly Monday press conference with football coach Ron Zook.

The UI sports information department provides detailed information about the teams in the upcoming contest. Sheppard sorts out what

Jim goes over final player scoring after the Illini basketball team beat Iowa 74-70 on Jan. 10, 2007, at the Assembly Hall.

Jim's photo from his senior year in high school at Fisher.

JIM SHEPPARD'S MILESTONE MOMENTS IN
BASKETBALL ANNOUNCING:

1) Jan. 21, 1993: Illinois 82, Penn State 66. Lou Henson's 600th career victory came in Penn State's first visit to the Assembly Hall. Henson was the 16th coach to reach that plateau.

2) Dec. 8, 1999: Illinois 98, Texas-Pan American 61. It was Lon Kruger's 63rd win at Illinois, but more importantly, the 300th of his career.

3) Dec. 30, 2005: Illinois 84, Tennesee-Martin 46. With 10:51 remaining in the second half, James Augustine grabbed his 11th rebound to become the Illini's career leader with 854. He passed Efrem Winters for the No. 1 spot. Augustine's career rebounding record stands at 1,023.

4) Dec. 3, 2006: Illinois 87, IUPUI 59. Coach Bruce Weber recorded his 200th career victory.

5) Jan. 6, 2007: Weber was presented the game ball from the 73-70 win against Missouri on Dec. 19, 2006, which made him the fastest coach in Big Ten history to reach 100 wins while at a conference school. The triumph occurred in his 118th game with the Illini.

will be most useful for him.

"As I prepare my sheets for the (football) game, I list the names and numbers for all of the offensive skill positions, quarterbacks, runners and receivers, plus the kickers, snappers, holders and kick-return personnel."

Notably absent are the offensive linemen, "because they seldom touch the ball. If an offensive lineman recovers a fumble, I refer to the complete team roster," he said.

His sheet also includes a numeric list of the first- and second-team defensive players. Since most visiting schools' press guides include a phonetic pronunciation guide, Sheppard said, they become "my Bible on game days for correctly pronouncing the challenging players' names."

Sheppard also tracks down the names of the captains for the game and announces them prior to the opening kickoff.

There are always special announcements to be read and the UI marketing department faxes them to Sheppard the night before so he can become familiar with what he is to say.

"I'm in the press box no later than two hours before kickoff," he said. "I always meet with the opponent's media contact to double-check names, uniform numbers and pronunciations."

Sheppard said there's an open door to his booth if an error is heard.

"I want the media contact to come into the public address booth and tell me if I mispronounce a player's name so I can correct my mistake," Sheppard said.

The pregame process is time-consuming, but Sheppard refuses to take shortcuts in football or basketball.

"There is no substitution for being prepared when announcing," he said.

Jim — in a stylish Roy Rogers robe —
enjoys Christmas in 1955 with sister Mary Jane.

JIM SHEPPARD'S FAVORITE BASKETBALL ARENAS OUTSIDE CHAMPAIGN:

1) Conseco Fieldhouse, Indianapolis. Neat looking building and very fan-friendly.
2) United Center, Chicago. Easy parking and the Michael Jordan statue is still impressive.
3) Mackey Arena, West Lafayette, Ind. The seats are close to the court and the place really rocks when the Illini visit.
4) Assembly Hall, Bloomington, Ind. Seats down low are OK; up high, bring the oxygen.
5) Redbird Arena, Normal, Ill. Even though the Illini haven't played there, I like the building.

CHAPTER 6

Tab Bennett and former assistant UI Sports Information Director Dale Ratermann turned to Sheppard following a tip from one of his broadcasting buddies, Bob Appuhn, from Danville radio station WDAN.

Appuhn and Sheppard had broadcast numerous high school games for their respective stations — Sheppard had started at Champaign's WDWS — and the two had developed a close association.

Both also had UI connections.

"When (former UI athletic director) Neale Stoner signed the first radio exclusive contract with Anheuser-Busch in the early 1980s, the initial plan was for me to be part of the broadcast with Dick Martin," Appuhn said. "However, the Cardinals' local affiliate (in Danville), WITY, told Anheuser-Busch they would not allow me on their airwaves, so I was blacklisted out of a statewide network because of a local situation."

That did not sit well with Appuhn.

"Since I grew up in DuQuoin as a Cardinals fan, and drank Budweiser, that was a real bitter moment for me on all levels," he added.

He had another chance for involvement at Illinois when Ratermann called and informed Appuhn of two game day openings.

"One was the official correspondent for any network or big-station markets (such as KMOX in St. Louis or WGN in Chicago) wanting reports and updates on games," Appuhn said.

"The other was the P.A. announcer."

It didn't take Appuhn long to make his choice.

"Illinois was a contender in both football and basketball, so I knew there would be lots of requests for those types of updates, which there were," he said. "Plus, I never had a comfort level doing P.A. work."

Appuhn accepted the correspondent's position, which he held for three years until 1988 when he moved to Logan, Utah, to handle play-by-play for Utah State.

"Dale asked who I would recommend for the P.A. job and the first name that came to mind was Jim Sheppard," Appuhn said.

Shortly thereafter, Ratermann left Illinois for a job with the Indiana Pacers and Bennett completed the deal with Sheppard to fill the void.

"That's how it all started for Jim and the Illini," Appuhn said. "Shep and I were intrinsically intertwined. We'd first met at a Monday UI football press conference in 1977 (eight years earlier) and had gotten to be fairly good friends."

Appuhn eventually had the chance to hear Sheppard over the loudspeaker and without his headphones on.

"My daughter (Katharine) went to school there and I sat in the stands four years at Dad's Day," Appuhn said, "and I think Jim does a fine job."

The UI P.A. opportunity marked the second time that Appuhn was a catalyst in getting Sheppard a job.

Their association began in 1977 at a high school football game between Champaign Central and Danville, a contest where Appuhn said, "the finish became a legend."

Danville defeated the Maroons, he recalled, "on the last play when Central kicked a ground ball to the quarterback in the middle of the field. He lateraled to a wideout, who ran it down the sidelines for the winning score.

"To this day, Champaign people will tell you it was an illegal forward pass."

The clip was included in an audio section of a 2004 book written by Fowler Connell, the longtime Danville Commercial-News sports editor.

"You can hear Jim's call behind mine," Appuhn said. "It was the kind of game where maybe 3,000 people were there, but ask around and it'll sound more like 30,000 today."

In 1978, Appuhn's duties at WDAN expanded and he began broadcasting UI games home and away.

"We needed someone who could do Danville games when I was traveling and we were also looking for another sales rep," Appuhn said. "Jim was mainly on-air at WDWS (doing limited ad sales), and I knew he was looking to do something else."

Appuhn mentioned Sheppard's name to the WDAN general manager, Joe Jackson, who made the hire.

While colleagues, Sheppard and Appuhn shared many memorable moments.

"When Purdue played at Illinois in 1980, NBC Radio called (WDAN) and asked us to do drop-ins for their hourly sportscasts,"

Appuhn said. "We worked it out that I did two when I was not on the air doing play-by-play and Jim did the other two when I was.

"He was working as my spotter then. The talent fee was $50. NBC never sent the money, and a few years later Jim moved to Indianapolis. Every time we spoke, the running joke was always, 'Where's my $25?' "

About three years later, NBC contacted Appuhn about getting another feed from the UI press box.

"I told the guy they still owed me $50 from 1980," Appuhn said. "Incredulous, he looked it up and it was actually still on file."

The check was put in the mail and, the following weekend, when Appuhn and Sheppard got together at Indianapolis for the Indy 500 time trials, "without saying a word, I took out my wallet, peeled off $25 and handed it to him," Appuhn said. "After a long, hard laugh, that money was put to good use later that evening."

JIM SHEPPARD'S CHILDHOOD DREAM JOBS:

1) Sports announcer: "Like so many young kids, who always liked sports, growing up to be a sports announcer was the ultimate," Sheppard said. "I did my first football game (for WDWS) in 1967 when Champaign Central played at Streator. Streator's coach was Joe Hall, who lettered at Illinois as a center in 1950 and 1952. Champaign Central was led by Tommy Stewart, a quarterback who lettered four years for Illinois from 1946 to '49. Tommy is a good friend whom I enjoyed working with. He sits in the booth next to me during Illini games today."

2) Sports writer: "Growing up, I knew I wanted to do something in the sports field. If I couldn't enter the announcing profession, I thought being a sports writer would be a good job. I was sports editor for my high school paper. Covering the basketball games was especially easy because I seldom got any playing time," Sheppard said. "The view from the end of the bench proved to be an editorial plus. I admire the writing skills of the individuals who cover sports at The News-Gazette today."

3) Pharmacist: "As a kid growing up in Fisher, I would often visit the local drug store to browse through the sports magazines. I got to know the pharmacists and was kind of fascinated by what they did," Sheppard said. "Sometimes they let me stand behind the counter and watch as they filled the prescriptions. The thought of becoming one of them didn't last long, as my interest in sports always resurfaced."

CHAPTER 7

Sheppard traces the beginning of his UI announcing duties to a football game on Sept. 7, 1985. The Illini were playing Southern Cal. The pregame hype had this showdown billed as a possible Rose Bowl preview.

The talent on both sides was superlative.

"I wasn't really concerned about doing my first game as the new Illini P.A. announcer and talking to 76,000-plus fans," Sheppard said. "I was just wondering what the new routine was going to be."

Intermingled with his eagerness to start was a sense of sadness that made for a bittersweet occasion.

"My father, Lyle, had passed away two years earlier from cancer and I thought about him that day and how I wished he could have been in the Memorial Stadium stands," Sheppard said.

The Trojans, ranked sixth nationally, beat the Illini 20-10.

Jim's parents Lucille and Lyle Sheppard in 1942, left, and 1980, below.

"It was a very hot day," Sheppard recalled.

Illinois' Jack Trudeau was hot as well, completing 21 of 37 passes for 310 yards. David Williams, who later was enshrined in the College Football Hall of Fame, hauled in eight of the completions for 112 yards.

Sheppard's tenure at Memorial Stadium is the second longest since the school introduced an electronic public address system on Oct. 2, 1926. He followed Tom Trent, who served in a similar capacity for six seasons. The longest tenure belonged to brothers Tiz and Paul Bresee, whose 37 seasons lasted from 1934 to '70. Fred Schooley then served for seven consecutive years.

Former Illini Ted Beach sent Sheppard a letter with a story regarding the Bresee brothers doing the P.A. at an unidentified game in the 1930s.

"Ted remembers a game where one of the brothers, Paul or Tiz, said, 'Penalty on Michigan for having an illegitimate receiver downfield,' and 70,000 fans yelled, 'Throw the bastard out.' "

The original P.A. announcer, according to Mike Pearson — who researched the subject for his book, "Illini Legends, Lists & Lore" — was Ted Canty. He handled the job for eight seasons, starting with Illinois' 27-0 victory against Coe College on Oct. 2, 1926.

Sheppard was high atop Memorial Stadium in 1985 for six home UI football games. Eighty days after he made his gridiron debut, he doubled his P.A. duties by sitting courtside at the Assembly Hall when the Illini faced Loyola in the men's basketball opener.

"I remember very little about the game," Sheppard confessed.

What stands out most is a chance pregame meeting with an Assembly Hall worker.

"As I was starting down the stairs toward the court, I remember the employee asking who I was," Sheppard said.

After Sheppard responded, he was greeted by the comment, "You have some big shoes to fill."

The Illini-Loyola game — won by Illinois in a runaway 95-64 — was the first that decade where the popular Tom Trent had not been behind the microphone.

Illinois' 1985 team centered around Glynn Blackwell, Bruce Douglas, Scott Meents, Ken Norman, Anthony Welch, Efrem Winters and Tony Wysinger.

Sheppard said he does not prefer working one sport over the other, but took note of one major difference.

"Because of my seat at the scorer's table at the Assembly Hall, you certainly feel more part of the game in basketball," he said. "However, when fans react to my announcements at the Stadium, that does make you feel like you're a part of the action.

"Both sports have their own unique feels and atmospheres."

Jim with long-time friend and spotter Rich Piccioli, left,
in the Memorial Stadium press box.

CHAPTER 8

Sheppard is not alone in the P.A. booth for football games at Memorial Stadium.

He is usually joined by four other people, two of whom are offensive spotter Rich Piccioli and defensive spotter Marc Czajkowski. Piccioli sits to the left of Sheppard and Czajkowski sits to Sheppard's right.

The duties of the offensive spotter are to inform Sheppard of the ball carrier or pass receiver and other important information concerning the offense.

"Rich wears a headset and communicates with the stat crew located in the booth next to us in the press box," Sheppard said. "He keeps track of the down and yardage on each play. He is also in communication with our on-the-field spotter, Lynn Sweet."

If the crew in the booth is unable to identify a player who recovers a fumble or blocks a punt, Piccioli speaks with Sweet and he finds out the needed information from the team.

"Rich has been in the booth with me all of the years I've announced and does a superb job," Sheppard said.

The duties of the defensive spotter are to tell Sheppard which players are making tackles. He also answers the emergency telephone in the booth.

"Occasionally, there are people who need to be paged during a game for emergency reasons," Sheppard said. "Marc will write down the information, hand it to me and I will announce it.

"He is a good friend who does a great job."

Also in the booth is Chris Hanna, the sales and marketing director for University of Illinois athletics. He directs the announcements that Sheppard reads during a game as well as what messages are shown on the stadium's scoreboard. He stands directly behind Sheppard in the booth.

The other person is either Bob Phillippe or C.V. Lloyde. They control all of the sound sources throughout the stadium, the public address system, the on-field microphones and the band.

"They are true professionals and do a great job," Sheppard said.

Piccioli has worked with Sheppard since the second game of his P.A. tenure in 1985.

Though they are friends away from the game, there is no time to socialize once they get to the P.A. booth.

"Jim is pretty intense," Piccioli said, "and very detailed. We have to concentrate and not get emotionally involved."

There's no time for idle chit-chat.

"I'll pick up the ball carrier's number, Marc gets the tacklers and I'm in communication with the stat box to our right and they give me the plus or minus yardage total," Piccioli said. "We get all that to Jim within 15 to 20 seconds, and then it's time for the next play."

Piccioli has no plans to leave his unpaid position soon.

"I will do it for as long as Jim does it," he said, "but we have a standing joke: Which will go first, my eyes or his voice?"

As for the P.A. job, Sheppard has a vision of how the position should be handled and he strives to meet his goal each game.

"In my opinion, a public address announcer needs to be precise with the information he gives during a game," Sheppard said. "He needs to be short and to the point.

"Everyone knows that homefield and the homecourt advantage can be huge in deciding the outcome of games. The home team public address announcer needs to know how to work the home crowd, but do it tastefully and never be disrespectful to the opposition.

"I've tried to develop my own style that excites Illini fans and makes the games exciting, but never to the point that I'm screaming or unprofessional. I do not appreciate P.A. voices that are 'homers,' uncontrollable in their delivery, and talk too much."

JIM SHEPPARD'S FAVORITE MOVIES:	
Dr. Zhivago	I saw it eight times and liked everything about it.
Shadowlands	A very moving picture with one of my favorites, Anthony Hopkins.
Forrest Gump	This is one in a long list of entertaining Tom Hanks movies I've enjoyed.
In The Heat of the Night	The performances by Sidney Poitier and Rod Steiger were great.
Serpico	How can you not enjoy Al Pacino's acting?

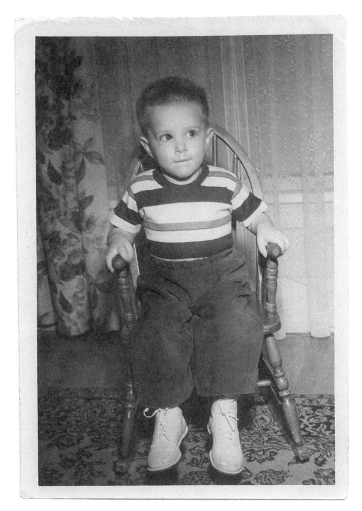

Jim ponders his future at a young age.

CHAPTER 9

The 1985 UI football team, coached by Mike White, held a unique distinction at the season's end. Among the starters were Jack Trudeau, the school's all-time passing yards leader (8,725), David Williams, the career receiving yards leader (3,392), Thomas Rooks, the career rushing yards leader (2,887), and hometown product Chris White, the coach's son and the career scoring leader (262 points).

More than two decades later, their legacy is becoming legend. Trudeau, Williams and White still rank No. 1 and Rooks has only fallen to No. 3.

The career rushing leader is Robert Holcombe, who gained 4,105 yards, and stands out as one of Sheppard's favorite football players.

"I admired his quiet strength, in addition to his football talents," Sheppard said.

Holcombe hit his rushing milestone in the 1997 season opener at home against Southern Mississippi. It was the first game of his senior season.

"The rugged ball carrier from Mesa, Ariz., needed just 36 yards to become the most prolific running back in Illinois history," Sheppard said. "Holcombe got the coveted record on a 5-yard burst up the middle early in the second quarter."

Though Sheppard told the crowd the significance of the carry, the game was not stopped nor was the game ball presented to Holcombe.

The only fanfare was provided by Sheppard's announcement: "Robert Holcombe has just become the all-time leading rusher in Illinois football history with 2,888 yards, breaking Thomas Rooks' record of 2,887, set from 1982 to 1985. Again, Robert Holcombe has now rushed

---

JIM SHEPPARD'S FAVORITE UI BASKETBALL GAMES HE SAW BUT DID NOT ANNOUNCE:

1) April 4, 2005: The NCAA championship game against North Carolina at the Edward Jones Dome in St. Louis. It was a disappointing 75-70 loss to the Tar Heels, but what fun we had getting there. That is a season Illini fans will never forget.

2) March 3, 2004: At Purdue, in West Lafayette, Ind., Luther Head tipped in a Roger Powell, Jr. miss with 0.9 second left in the first overtime period and then intercepted Purdue's last-chance attempt moments later. The Illini won 81-79 and clinched at least a share of the Big Ten title in coach Bruce Weber's first season in Champaign. Four days later, the Illini knocked off Ohio State in Columbus 64-63 to win the outright conference championship.

3) January 11, 1979: At the Assembly Hall against Michigan State. The Illini entered the game with a 14-0 record while the Spartans were ranked No. 1 in the country. The rest is history. Eddie Johnson hit a baseline jumper in the closing seconds and the Illini nipped MSU and Magic Johnson 57-55.

4) January 28, 1984: At the Assembly Hall against Michigan. The fans got their money's worth in this one. A four-overtime battle was won by the Illini 75-66. Illinois tied for the Big Ten title that season with a league record of 15-3 for coach Lou Henson's only championship in his 21 years at Illinois.

5) March 18, 1989: Against Ball State at the Indianapolis Hoosier Dome. Ball State was undefeated and ranked No. 18 in the country when the two teams met in the Midwest Regional final of the NCAA tournament. The Illini won 72-60 to advance to Minneapolis, where they played Louisville.

for 36 yards today and 2,888 in his Illinois career, making him the all-time career rushing leader at Illinois."

Entering the 2007 season, Holcombe's standard is still the mark all backs at the school are shooting for. Others in the top five are: Antoineo Harris, 2,985 yards from 1999-2002; Thomas Rooks, 2,887 yards from 1982-85; Jim Grabowski, 2,878 yards from 1963-65 and Rocky Harvey, 2,711 yards from 1998-2001.

"I have always thought that Holcombe's record was overshadowed by that season, Ron Turner's first at Illinois," Sheppard said.

The Illini lost the '97 opener to Southern Mississippi 24-7 and finished the season 0-11.

In his first year doing the P.A. at Illini football games, Sheppard found a time when the best policy was to say nothing.

Illinois was playing Ohio State and Chris White was preparing for a field goal with the game tied 28-28.

"I announced Chris White's name as he lined up for the late field goal attempt," Sheppard said. "After the Buckeyes called time out, trying to put more pressure on White, I turned to spotter Rich Piccioli and he said, 'Don't announce Chris' name again.'

"I thought Rich's suggestion was a good one, so I did not. At that moment, silence was golden. I didn't want to put any more pressure on Chris and repeating the situation might have taken away the magic.

"Moments later, White's kick sailed through the south uprights and Memorial Stadium exploded. After the game, those of us in the public address booth celebrated as well. It was a tremendous Fighting Illini victory."

Piccioli said his thinking was that the announcement had already been made, plus "let's not jinx him," he said. "Everyone knew what was going on."

Jim meeting Little Oscar, left, from Oscar Mayer, in 1958.

JIM SHEPPARD'S BIG-HEARTED PLAYERS HE ADMIRES:

"One of the aspects of sports that has always intrigued me is the mental side of competition and teams with their backs to the wall that come together on a given day and pull off upsets," Sheppard said. "I enjoy athletes who play with big hearts, fierce determination and mental toughness. Here are some of the UI athletes I've watched over the years that I have a lot of respect for."

BASKETBALL

NAME	YEARS	SHEPPARD'S COMMENT
Dee Brown	2003-06	The gas that made the Illini engine go.
Chester Frazier	2007-current	Never lets pain get in his way.
Matt Heldman	1995-98	Directed Lon Kruger's co-championship club in 1997-98.
Lucas Johnson	1999-2002	Not the most talented, but few matched his reckless toughness.
Sergio McClain	1998-2001	A winner in every sense.

FOOTBALL

NAME	YEARS	SHEPPARD'S COMMENT
Eric Guenther	1995-97, 99	Soft-spoken gentleman off the field, but watch out when the pads go on.
Robert Holcombe	1994-97	Had a quiet strength about himself.
Kurt Kittner	1998-2001	Low-key leader who hung out with his offensive line buddies.
J Leman	2004-07	Interesting character who has turned into one of the country's premier linebackers.
Josh Norris	2004-06	Got the most out of his abilities.

CHAPTER 10

One of Sheppard's toughest football games to work came on Sept. 22, 2001, 11 days after the terrorist attack on the World Trade Center in New York City.

The Illini game against Louisville had been postponed from Sept. 15.

Memorial Stadium was instead the site for a community-wide remembrance on Sept. 15, one which Sheppard said was designed to "bring some sort of comfort to all of us."

It was a tremendous time of national mourning and athletic contests were not first and foremost in anyone's thoughts.

"I personally supported the decision to reschedule the Illinois-Louisville game and others around the country," Sheppard said. "As the next week unfolded, I think people were trying to resume their normal daily lives and get back to a routine of some sort.

"I was ready, as difficult as it was, to start thinking about a football game again."

Sheppard, whose astrological sign is Libra, didn't consult the stars for signs on how to proceed.

"Once in a while, I'll read what kind of day I'm supposed to have," he said, "but I don't put any stock in what it says.

"I always try to begin each day with a positive attitude and make the best of whatever happens."

On Sept. 22, he rode the elevator to the broadcasting booth high atop the west side of Memorial Stadium and did what he had grown accustomed to doing for years.

"I was able to focus on my announcing job and do everything as normal as possible," he said.

It was just a new normal. For everyone.

Though the vast majority of his announcements are positive and uplifting, a few are somber in nature. Sheppard said one of his hardest moments in basketball occurred on Dec. 9, 2000, when the Illini were playing Seton Hall.

At the eight-minute mark of the first half, he was asked to read this announcement:

"Please direct your attention to halfcourt for a special presentation. I remember like it was yesterday, saying these

Jim reading final announcements after an Illini game at Assembly Hall.

words, 'That's a three, Matt Heldman.' Fourteen months ago, Matthew Heldman, point guard for the 1997-98 Big Ten championship team, was tragically killed in an auto accident in Chicago.

"To perpetuate his memory and provide support for the Illinois basketball program, Orange Krush has pledged to raise $250,000 to endow a scholarship for future Illinois basketball players.

"Here today to present the first installment of $40,000 for the Orange Krush Matthew Heldman Memorial Scholarship Fund are Jared Gelfond, Chip Jorstad and Lindsay Nance. Accepting the check on behalf of the Division of Intercollegiate Athletics is Director of Athletics Ron Guenther.

"This incredible support by University students is truly a unique program and a first in Fighting Illini Scholarship Fund history. Let's give a big round of applause for all the members of the Orange Krush for their hard work and outstanding Illinois loyalty. Go Illini!"

Sheppard said he was aware of the atmosphere inside the Assembly Hall as he read the announcement.

"It was extremely quiet and very emotional," he said.

In 2002, Illinois basketball created the Matto Award in memory of Matt Heldman.

The winners to date:

2002 Lucas Johnson	2003 Dee Brown	2004 Dee Brown
2005 Dee Brown	2006 Dee Brown	2007 Chester Frazier

Former UI point guard Matt Heldman,
who died in an October 1999 auto accident.

CHAPTER 11

Sheppard has not consciously tried to emulate any of the great broadcasters or P.A. announcers of the past century, though the life-long sports fan has heard his share of outstanding ones.

"I've admired and listened to several announcers over the years," he said. "The first sports announcer I really remember well was Jack Quinlan, radio voice of the Chicago Cubs during parts of the 1950s and 1960s."

Quinlan died in an automobile accident during spring training in 1965.

"I've never incorporated any phrases or announcing styles from others," Sheppard said. "I feel broadcasters and public address announcers should develop their own niche and feel comfortable with what they're doing.

"I'm not aware of any other announcer copying me."

Sheppard was raised in Fisher, located in northwest Champaign

County, about 20 minutes from Champaign-Urbana. His interest in sports took hold at a young age.

"One of my childhood memories was taking my empty pop bottles down to Heiser & Ingold's grocery store in Fisher, receiving five cents a bottle and then buying baseball cards with that sweet powdery bubble gum.

"I'd sit on empty milk cartons in the back of the store listening to WGN and Quinlan. As I started to follow the Illini, I would tune in Larry Stewart on the Purity Sunbeam Network in Champaign. On

---

JIM SHEPPARD'S FAVORITE UI FOOTBALL GAMES HE SAW BUT DID NOT ANNOUNCE:

1) October 23, 1999: At Michigan. The Illini successfully rally from a 20-point deficit. Rocky Harvey scored the last two touchdowns, including the famous dive-into-the-end-zone score. Illinois wins 35-29.

2) December 30, 1999: Against Virginia in Miami. The Micronpc.com Bowl game at Pro Player Stadium saw the Illini accumulate the second-highest point total in bowl game history while crushing the Cavaliers 63-21. Kurt Kittner threw for 254 yards and also caught a 30-yard touchdown pass from Brandon Lloyd.

3) November 13, 1999: At Ohio State. The Illini gave the Buckeyes one of their worst home losses in history, 46-20. That year marked the first time in history that Illinois defeated both Ohio State and Michigan on the road in the same season.

   As my wife, Joan, and I stood outside the Illini locker room waiting to congratulate the players and coaches, long lines of saddened Buckeye fans walked by, many holding big chunks of the Ohio Stadium turf. The major upgrade work on the grand old stadium was starting that very afternoon.

   When Joan and I moved outside the stadium and waited to say hi to Brian (Scott, my stepson) and the other players before they boarded the buses, we saw coach Ron Turner being stopped by Ohio state troopers on his way to the bus. They wanted his autograph.

4) October 3, 1959: At Memorial Stadium against Army. It was the first Illini game I saw in person and Illinois beat the fourth-ranked Cadets 20-14 in Ray Eliot's last season as the UI head coach. The Army team featured Bill Carpenter, dubbed the Lonesome End. The Illini star was Bill Burrell, a guard and linebacker, who finished fourth in the Heisman Trophy voting that season.

5) January 1, 1990: Against Virginia in Orlando. In the Florida Citrus Bowl, Jeff George completed 26 of 38 passes for 321 yards and three touchdowns. It was the last game in George's career at Illinois and he was chosen the game's Most Valuable Player as the Illini won 31-21.

Jim poses with the Illini Sports Network broadcasting team, back row, from left, Loren Tate, Steve Kelly and Brian Barnhart.

television, it was always Tom Schoendienst on WCIA Channel 3."

Sheppard didn't just show up one day at the University of Illinois and talk to Tab Bennett about the P.A. positions. He'd already had experience in a related field.

After graduating from Fisher High School in 1966, he enrolled at a broadcasting school in Milwaukee. That fall, he was hired as a staff announcer at Champaign radio station WDWS.

"A year later, the station's general manager, Larry Stewart, gave me my first opportunity to do play-by-play and I covered local and area high school football and basketball games," Sheppard said.

While employed at the station, Sheppard would frequently accompany Stewart and legendary former coach Ray Eliot on road trips to UI football games. For years, Stewart was known as the "Voice of the Illini" for those who followed the UI teams via the radio.

JIM SHEPPARD'S MOST MEMORABLE ILLINI FOOTBALL GAMES FOR YEARS HE ANNOUNCED:

1) Oct. 5, 1985: Vs. Ohio State. Chris White drills a field goal with under a minute to play as the Illini edge the Buckeyes 31-28.

2) Nov. 5, 1988: Vs. Indiana. Hoosiers lead Illini by 11 points with less than four minutes left. Many fans had left the stadium thinking Indiana would win. Jeff George finds Mike Bellamy in the north end zone for the game-winner. Final: Illinois 21, Indiana 20.

3) Sept. 23, 2000: Vs. Michigan. A year after the Illini had stunned the Wolverines in Ann Arbor, Michigan meets Illinois in a sold-out night game at Memorial Stadium. Thanks to controversial fumble calls that went against the Illini late in the game, the Wolverines hang on for a 35-31 victory.

4) Nov. 12, 1994: Vs. Penn State. Illini led the second-ranked Nittany Lions 21-0 at the half, but quarterback Kerry Collins rallies Penn State to a 35-31 victory.

5) Nov. 22, 2001: Vs. Northwestern. Thanksgiving Day. Illinois beats state rival 34-28 to win its first outright Big Ten championship since 1983. Coach Ron Turner's team is ranked 12th in the final Associated Press poll.

6) Sept. 15, 1990: Vs. Colorado. The Illini open the season at Arizona and lose 28-16. Next is the home opener against the No. 11 Buffaloes. Illinois nips Colorado 23-22. Colorado wins the rest of its games that season and captures the national championship.

7) Nov. 4, 2006: Vs. Ohio State. Illinois battles the top-ranked Buckeyes as well as any team does all season, but Ohio State wins 17-10. It was the closest game of the season for the Buckeyes, who went on to play in the national title game.

8) Sept. 4, 1999: Vs. Arkansas State. Stepson and senior offensive center Brian Scott sees his first Illini action, replacing the injured Luke Butkus, and Illinois wins the season opener 41-3.

9) Sept. 3, 2005: Vs. Rutgers. Illini rally to win in overtime 33-30 in Ron Zook's first game. The game-winner was a 2-yard run by Pierre Thomas.

10) Sept. 20, 1986: Vs. Nebraska. The Cornhuskers crush the Illini in a night game 59-14. At halftime, Dick Butkus' uniform No. 50 is retired.

11) Sept. 22, 1990: Vs. Southern Illinois. Howard Griffith scores eight touchdowns to set an NCAA record. The Illini roll to a 56-21 win.

12) Sept. 6, 2003: Vs. Illinois State. Illinois beats the Redbirds 49-22 for its only win of the season. Rantoul product and former Illini Dwayne Smith turns in the greatest receiving performance in Memorial Stadium history with 13 receptions, 243 yards and two TDs.

13) Sept. 7, 1985: Vs. Southern Cal. My first game as public address announcer. Trojans beat the Illini 20-10. Coach Mike White's squad ends the season 6-5-1, his last winning record at Illinois.

14) Sept. 1, 1994: Vs. Washington State. Game played at Chicago's Soldier Field. Crowd of 39,472 watches Illini drop a 10-9 decision. Simeon Rice sets a standing school record with five quarterback sacks.

15) Sept. 20, 2003: Vs. California. A record-setting day for UI quarterback Jon Beutjer, but the Illini lose 31-24. Beutjer throws for the most yards of anyone in Memorial Stadium history, 430. He completes 35 of 57 passes, three for touchdowns.

"In those days, we drove to Saturday football games played at Northwestern, Indiana and Purdue," Sheppard said. "It was a thrill for me to ride on those trips with Stewart and Eliot.

"I had listened to Stewart for years growing up as a kid and Eliot was his color sidekick. The stories I heard from Eliot about his former players and the Rose Bowl teams were something special for me at that young age."

The subject wasn't always a bygone era. Occasionally, Stewart provided tips to his young protégé.

"He told me to frequently tell the listeners the score and the time remaining," Sheppard said.

As he gained experience in the broadcast booth, there were no critiques from Stewart.

"I just learned as I went and listened to my games on tape to correct my errors," Sheppard said.

Jim with Lynette Woodard, the first woman to play for the Harlem Globetrotters. Woodard was signed on Oct. 7, 1985.

When the opportunity arose, Sheppard tried to learn from those around him.

"Whenever I went to other arenas and stadiums, I listened very carefully to the P.A. announcer and how he handled the pronunciations," Sheppard said. "I've always put extra effort at games I've announced into pronouncing the players' names correctly."

Sheppard's decision to pursue broadcasting seemed natural during his teenage years.

"I always enjoyed sports," he said. "Little League baseball, backyard Whiffleball games, shooting baskets, neighborhood football games, the typical stuff kids do.

Jim poses with Illini linebackers Dana Howard, left, and John Holecek.

"I remember I would announce as I played those games and so I started thinking about being an announcer."

He funneled that interest into duties as the sports editor of his high school paper. By then, however, Sheppard knew he wouldn't be making a living by playing sports.

"I participated throughout high school and was a very average athlete," Sheppard said.

One highlight from his career at the school with the famed mascot — the Bunnies — was being the varsity center on a football team which compiled a 7-2 record.

"Looking back, we would have easily made the playoffs if they had been in existence," said Sheppard, who graduated eight years before the Illinois High School Association instituted the postseason playoff format in football.

Sheppard has found that folks outside of central Illinois can identify with Fisher.

"People may not know where Fisher is, but they know the Bunnies," he said. "The only other high school in the country with Bunnies as the nickname is in Omaha, Neb."

The acknowledgement of Bunnies as the school moniker came into existence when Sheppard's father, Lyle, attended the high school.

"My father was a member of the 1933-34 basketball team when the nickname was created by (Champaign-Urbana) News-Gazette sports writer Eddie Jacquin."

The story goes that Jacquin noticed some of the players attached rabbit feet to their belts. He commented that they looked like bunnies. The reference stuck.

Young Jim filling up the gas tank in 1960.
Gas prices then: 30 cents
Gas prices in 2007: $3.00

CHAPTER 12

Much of Sheppard's adult life has been spent in sports or advertising sales.

In the fall of 1966, he became a staff announcer at WDWS, the flagship station of the Fighting Illini. He handled high school football and basketball broadcasts, helped out with the Illinois broadcasts and broke into advertising sales.

"I enjoyed my early years in radio, but knew I eventually wanted to move into a bigger market," Sheppard said.

After a 12-year stint at WDWS, he moved to Danville radio station WDAN, he said to "work more in ad sales." During his three years in Vermilion County, Sheppard's emphasis was in ad sales, but he continued to do high school play-by-play.

"The move to WDAN was good for me personally for two reasons," Sheppard said. "One, I could increase my income because I could spend more time selling advertising, which I enjoyed. And two, I could still be involved with play-by-play sports, which I also enjoyed.

"I've always been a stickler for details. A parallel between working in ad sales and doing public address work is that both positions require a certain level of being organized and effectively managing your advertising accounts or the information used in announcing games."

Jim visits the NFL Hall of Fame in Canton, Ohio.

Jim meets up with former Illini All-American and current NFL star Simeon Rice.

At WDAN, Sheppard made a favorable impression with his co-workers, including Jeanne Eisenhauer, who started at the station in 1959 and officially retired in 1997 but continues in 2007 to do a weekly one-hour Saturday morning show for master gardeners.

"Jim was a perfectionist and was known as 'Mr. Clean,' " Eisenhauer said. "His desk was spotless. That would be the first thing he'd do every morning, make sure everything was in its place and that everything had a place. He was so precise and neat.

"When he'd leave to go out on calls, if he had a note on his desk, it better not be moved or you'd be in trouble."

Eisenhauer's job was that of traffic director, which didn't mean she reported on rush-hour highway congestion.

"The traffic director is the person who puts all the commercials and programming on the logs for the announcers," Eisenhauer said.

She said typically the station's half-dozen salesmen would write up the commercials and "let Jeanne put them wherever she wanted to put them," following a few basic rules. "You had to make sure two restaurants weren't together. They had to be 15 minutes apart," she said.

Sheppard, however, didn't just turn in his ad and leave.

"He handed it to me and would stand over my shoulder to make sure I understood what he meant on every line, make sure I understood this is what the advertiser wanted," Eisenhauer said. "I could always

---

JIM SHEPPARD'S FAVORITE FOOTBALL STADIUMS OUTSIDE OF ILLINOIS:

1) Ohio Stadium, Columbus, Ohio: Magnificent venue that rings with tradition.
2) Camp Randall Stadium, Madison, Wis.: Badger fans really get into it. Parking leaves a lot to be desired.
3) Papa John's Cardinal Stadium, Louisville, Ky.: I was there in 1999 when the Illini won 41-36. You can buy a "cold one" there, too.
4) Memorial Stadium, Bloomington, Ind.: No bad seats in the place and there's lots of parking.
5) Kinnick Stadium, Iowa City, Iowa: The best thing is their large and loud score-board.

Announcing high above Zuppke Field from the Memorial stadium press box.

JIM SHEPPARD'S FAVORITE ILLINI TONGUE-TWISTERS FROM THE YEARS HE ANNOUNCED:

(listed alphabetically)

PLAYER	PHONETIC PRONUNCIATION	UI YEARS	SPORT
Ade Adeyemo	(AH-dee AH-dee-ah-mo)	2001, 2003-04	football
Nana Agyeman	(NAH-nuh ADJ-uh-men)	2000-02	football
Jon Asamoah	(ASS-uh-mow-uh)	2006-active	football
Peter Christofilakos	(KRISS-toe-fil-ah-kos)	2001-02	football
Victor Chukwudebe	(Chew-koo-day-bay)	1997-2000	basketball
Michael Cklamovski	(cluh-MAHV-skee)	2006-active	football
Mike Craciunoiu	(KRASS-in-oye)	1999	football
Cory Flisakowski	(FLIS-ah-cow-skee)	2001	football
Rich Gianacakos	(GEE-an-cock-os)	1990	football
Brian Grzelakowski	(GRIZ-lah-cow-skee)	2004-05	football
Michael Hoomanawanui	(huh-oh-muh-NOW-uh-noo-ee)	2006-active	football
Kyle Knezetic	(kuh-NEZ-uh-tick)	2004-active	football
Andy Kpedi	(PED-e)	1990-91	basketball
Damir Krupalija	(DA-mere CREW-paul-yuh)	1999-2002	basketball
Jens Kujawa	(Yens KOO-yah-wah)	1986-88	basketball
Dan Motuliak	(MOT-uh-lack)	2006-active	football
Mike Nabolotny	(NOB-uh-lot-knee)	2006-active	football
Fred Nkemdi	(N-kim-dee)	2004-05	basketball
Ray Redziniak	(RED-zin-e-ak)	1997-2000	football
Kyle Schnettgoecke	(SHNET-go-kee)	2005	football
Jeff Schwarzentraub	(SHWAR-zen-traub)	1993	football
Chris Siambekos	(SEE-am-beck-os)	1986, 1989	football

count on Jim being very precise."

Nearly three decades after Sheppard's departure from the station, Eisenhauer still has a tape of a commercial the two of them did.

"It was a 30-second commercial, but it took us 30 minutes to do it," she said. "Any time I am down in the dumps or feeling blue, all I have to do is drag out that CD."

The spot was for Giacomo's Deli, which is no longer in business.

"Something struck Jim as funny about the name 'Giacomo,' and when he started reading his part, he got tickled," Eisenhauer said. "It was a riot.

"If he didn't laugh, I would. We'd almost get to the end and start giggling. We were laughing so hard, we were crying, and we knew it was stupid, but once we got to laughing, we couldn't stop."

Eisenhauer recalled that Sheppard was insistent that he do the commercial and not let a colleague read the part.

"That was Jim's client and he wanted to do it," Eisenhauer said. "He had faith eventually we'd get through it."

Sheppard had a penchant for making certain everything was done as close to perfection as possible.

"The customer really got their money's worth when they had Jim as a salesman," Eisenhauer said. "He did everything he could to get the commercial just so.

"He was a perfectionist and yet, he had a sense of humor. He was a funny guy, but could be very serious. You had to love him."

While at WDAN, Sheppard crossed paths with John Eckert, who remembers his former co-worker as "an agreeable, hardworking colleague and always a gentleman. He was very pleasant and I remember well his resonant voice."

Incredibly, one of the sponsorship ads Sheppard sold and wrote while at WDAN is still in use more than a quarter of a century after his departure. It reads: "First Savings Bank on West Williams. First in Danville since 1880."

Mike Hulvey, the station manager, said the spot is read by news director Bill Pickett "at least three times a week," as an introduction to the newscast.

"We've edited the name of the bank (which was First Savings and Loan Association when Sheppard was in town), but otherwise, it has been untouched," Hulvey said.

Sheppard journeyed from Danville to Indianapolis, where he worked for country-formatted WFMS.

"That's when I was exposed to a higher level of media sales," he said. "I really enjoyed my years in Indiana's capital city, but returned to Champaign-Urbana in 1993."

Since then, he has worked in advertising sales, except for a two-year stint with a publishing company. He left WCIA television, where he was an ad representative, in 2001 for a position at The News-Gazette selling advertising in the official University of Illinois sports publications.

CHAPTER 13

Many in the sports broadcasting business seem to have catch-phrases or sayings for which they are remembered and revered for decades. Two words come to mind when people think about Hall of Fame baseball announcer Harry Caray: Holy Cow.

Sheppard will forever be linked to one saying as well, one which was not planned, but just seemed

"Holy Cow" what a picture! Jim with Cubs broadcasting icon Harry Caray.

to roll off his tongue when an Illini freshman Daniel "Dee" Brown buried a three-point shot in the opening minute of the second half of a Nov. 27, 2002, game against Arkansas-Pine Bluff.

"Deeeeeeeeeeee for threeeeeee," Sheppard gushed into the microphone to the delight of the Assembly Hall spectators and, ultimately, the freshman player himself.

"It was great," said former UI football coach Ron Turner, who watched many of the home basketball games, "that he tailored that call for Dee."

The trey against Arkansas-Pine Bluff was the second in the game for Brown, who ended the game 4 for 7 from beyond the 19-foot, 9-inch arc as the Illini won 96-43.

"Those sitting around me at the scorer's bench were a little surprised, but enjoyed it," Sheppard said. "I used the phrase for the rest of Brown's career at the Assembly Hall."

Brown's teammates were impressed with the call, too.

Jim with former Illini Dee Brown.

"That is going down in history as one of the greatest quotes an announcer could say," said Jerrance Howard, an Illini from 2001 to '04.

Brown's home era ended on Feb. 26, 2006, in a 71-59 triumph against Iowa. Fittingly, Sheppard was able to use his signature line "Deeeeeeeeeee for threeeeeee" twice in Brown's last home appearance.

"Dee has mentioned how he liked the phrase and that he wanted to make his three-point attempts to hear me say it," Sheppard said.

It caught on with fans as well.

"T-shirts were made and, to this day, people still remember 'Deeeeeeeeeeee for threeeeeee,'" Sheppard said.

Though Brown ultimately became enamored with the phase, at first it didn't catch his attention. Following the first game in which Sheppard said it, Brown told a News-Gazette reporter, "I've got to get back (downcourt) and be a general. I've got to tell my team what defense we're in. I'm not really listening to the announcer. You can't help but hear the crowd roaring, but ... I barely knew he was saying that."

It took a while before Brown was consumed by the hoopla surrounding the announcement about his perimeter shooting.

"I really didn't pay attention until everyone made it famous," he said. "It was great to hear that. It made me want to come out and play well and make shots."

Brown, who now plays for the NBA's Utah Jazz, said he is indebted to Sheppard.

"I think that Jim Sheppard did a good job of putting me out there and starting something real good for me," Brown said. "Sheppard is one of the best announcers ever, and he did a lot for my career. I want to thank him.

"I really appreciate him and have nothing but love for him. He's the best. That's pretty much all I can say."

Though Sheppard turned the phrase, Brown said there's one reason it caught on.

"We had great fans," Brown said. "I tried to get the crowd involved, and play well."

In his 137-game career with the Illini, Brown hit three-pointers in 120 games. Sixty-three of those games were played at the Assembly Hall or as a regular-season home game at the United Center. Sheppard was able to make his infamous call for Brown 151 times.

"I think 'Deeeeeeeeeeee for threeeeeee' kind of got tied in with the whole Dee persona: the high socks, the head band, the orange mouthpiece and then 'Deeeeeeeeeeee for threeeeeee,' " UI coach Bruce Weber said. "It really took off during the second half of Dee's junior year when he hit all of those threes and got hot down the stretch.

"Two games that specifically stand out were the final home game of Dee's junior year against Purdue and his senior year against Michigan State in the Big Ten opener. It just seemed like every time down the court you heard 'Deeeeeeeeeeee for threeeeeee.' "

One reason the rhyme was so effective, according to longtime associate UI athletic director Dana Brenner is Brown's proficiency for the shot.

"It was synonymous to Jim because of the repetitiveness of it," Brenner said. "If (Brown) were making one or two every other game, it probably wouldn't have had the same effect."

Even today, Weber can still hear the call, and not just in his mind.

"We even have it as part of our highlight tapes over the past few years," Weber said. "You can hear, 'Deeeeeeeeeeee for threeeeeee' or 'Thaaaaaaaaaat's a three' over the highlights."

CHAPTER 14

Sheppard's delivery on all three-pointers by the Illini — starting with "thaaaaaaaaaaat's a three" — was so memorable that it stayed with the players even when they played games without 16,000-plus spectators watching their every move.

"We would say it in practice, even in the summertime when somebody hit a game-winning three-pointer," ex-Illini Jerry Hester said. " 'Thaaaaaaaaaaat's a three' ... that line is a part of the Illinois tradition."

Hometown product Trent Meacham — who began attending Illini games when he was 3 — said in his formative years he would use that line himself.

"Growing up, I can remember shooting around in my back yard and yelling 'That's a three, Trent Meacham,' " said the Centennial High School graduate.

Robin Scholz/The News-Gazette

News-Gazette columnist Loren Tate talks with former Illini Jerry Hester before a game against Quincy University on November 9, 2005.

It was more of a thrill, he admitted, when he heard it from the source.

"It was pretty cool to hear him announce it this past season at the Assembly Hall," Meacham said. "It's really like a dream come true after all of those years saying it over and over in my head."

Former UI basketball players weren't the only ones who found the phrase sticking in their minds. It was also something former UI football coach Ron Turner retained.

"For myself, when I see a three-pointer — especially watching the Illini — I think of that call," Turner said.

As Sheppard settled into his P.A. work, he said he placed himself in the position of others.

"I asked myself, 'What information would I want to hear if I was a fan in the stands?' For those fans sitting high up in C section at the Assembly Hall, it would be hard at times to tell if a long field goal attempt made was a two-pointer or a three-pointer," he said.

"And so I created, with a little flair, 'Thaaaaaaaaaat's a three' ... Cory Bradford or Richard Keene or Luther Head or Sean Harrington (or whomever). Those players are four of the top five in school history in three-pointers.

"The other is Dee Brown, and you know what I announced for him."

Hester said he appreciated Sheppard's work while he played, but only since he joined WDWS' play-by-play announcer Brian Barnhart as the color commentator for UI broadcasts did he really get to know Sheppard.

"Being a player, you didn't really get the chance to know him personally," Hester said. "He was always upbeat and you could see the passion he had for doing the P.A., but you didn't know what kind of person he was.

ILLINOIS BASKETBALL LETTERMEN, 1985-2007:

Halim Abdullah 1997	Tim Geers 1990-91	Ken Norman 1985-87
Doug Altenberger 1985, '87	Ken Gibson 1990	Bryant Notree 1995-97
Nick Anderson 1988-89	Kendall Gill 1987-90	Scott Pierce 1991-92
Robert Archibald..1999-02	Jim Green 1987	Roger Powell Jr. .. 2002-05
Marcus Arnold 2006-07	Marcus Griffin 2000-01	Shaun Pruitt 2005-07
James Augustine . 2003-06	Lowell Hamilton ...1986-89	Brian Randle .. 2004, 06-07
Stephen Bardo 1987-90	Sean Harrington .. 2000-03	Brett Robisch 1995
Kenny Battle 1988-89	Davin Harris 1993	Steve Roth 1992-95
Robert Bennett 1992-95	Fess Hawkins 1999	Mark Shapland 1989
Rich Beyers 1998	Luther Head 2002-05	Ervin Small 1988-90
Glynn Blackwell ...1986-88	Matt Heldman 1995-98	Jamar Smith 2006-07
Ryan Blackwell 1996	Jerry Hester ...1994-96, 98	Larry Smith..... 1987-89, '91
Jelani Boline 1997-98	Chris Hicks 2007	Nick Smith 2002-05
P.J. Bowman 1989-90	Jerrance Howard .2001-04	Aaron Spears 2004
Cory Bradford 1999-02	Nick Huge 2003	Awvee Story 1998
Calvin Brock 2006-07	Jack Ingram 2004-05	Brooks Taylor 1990-93
Cleotis Brown 1999-00	C.J. Jackson 2006-07	Curtis Taylor 1986
Dee Brown 2003-06	Brian Johnson 1995-98	Clayton Thomas 2003
Herb Caldwell 1996-97	Lucas Johnson 1999-02	Deon Thomas 1991-94
Brian Carlwell 2007	Rodney Jones 1990	Derrick Thomas 1995
Warren Carter 2004-07	Andy Kaufmann ..1990-91; 93	Kevin Turner 1995-98
Victor Chukwudebe 1997-00	Richard Keene 1993-96	Will Tuttle 1992
Doug Clarida 1992	Charles Keller 1986	Anthony Welch 1985-86
Shelly Clark 1994-95	Andy Kpedi 1990-91	T.J. Wheeler 1992-94
Rennie Clemons ... 1991-93	Damir Krupalija 1999-02	Deron Williams 2003-05
Brian Cook 2000-03	Jens Kujawa 1986-88	Frank Williams 2000-02
Gene Cross 1993-94	Phil Kunz 1987-88	Kyle Wilson 2003
Joe Cross 2000-01	Marcus Liberty 1989-90	Efrem Winters 1985-86
Marc Davidson 1992-93	Ed Manzke 1989	Reggie Woodward 1986
Arias Davis 1998-99	Nate Mast 1999-01	Tony Wysinger 1985-87
Bruce Douglas 1985-86	Rich McBride 2004-07	
Mike Duis 1992	Sergio McClain 1998-01	NOTE: Some players in the
Blandon Ferguson 2002-03	Mike McDonald 1989	above list also lettered
Chester Frazier 2006-07	Trent Meacham 2007	prior to 1985, but the list is
David Freeman 1997-98	Scott Meents 1985-86	only intended to represent
Chris Gandy 1994-97	Brett Melton 2001	the athletes and the years
Kiwane Garris 1994-97	Tom Michael 1991-94	that Sheppard announced
Jarrod Gee 1995-98	Fred Nkemdi 2004-05	them.

ARE YOU READY?

"The last couple of years, eating dinner with him and talking to him after games, you see the type of person he is, very caring in general, not just for sports, but a real genuine person. He's a great guy to get to know.

"You know where you stand with Jim."

In retrospect, Hester recognizes how integral Sheppard was as a part of the UI program.

"I don't get the impression that most guys (at other schools) knew who their P.A. guy was," Hester said. "At Illinois, you can see where players would go up, including myself, and shake his hand or point at Jim."

Hester said it's difficult to compare Sheppard to the public address announcers he heard at other venues.

"On the road, you're so focused on the game and your opponent, you don't pay attention to anything else," said Hester, whose full-time job is as a financial representative for Northwest Mutual. "It's you against the world."

J Leman, the star linebacker from Champaign Central, said most of his knowledge about Sheppard came from the Illini games he attended while still in high school.

"I don't really hear that stuff when I'm playing," Leman said. "When you are locked in on the game, you don't hear the outside stuff."

In some respects, Sheppard is a background worker who has an essential role in the game.

"You don't come to the game to see the P.A. announcer, but you always remember him and his ability to get the info out," Hester said, "and Jim has coined a couple of phrases that fans remember.

"Twenty-two years in any profession is a long time when you're looking at people only staying nine or 10 years in a career."

For Sheppard, the feeling of admiration is mutual. When asked to pick his all-time favorite Illini five, he included Hester on his list.

"The list was not based on basketball skills only, but also on the players' personalities," Sheppard said. "Lists like this are hard to select because there are so many other favorite players as well."

Jim meets Chicago White Sox Hall of Famer Luke Appling.

CHAPTER 15

Not all of Sheppard's action has occurred in basketball. He was behind the microphone for the 1990 football game at Memorial Stadium
when Howard Griffith scored an NCAA-record eight touchdowns.

Many of the marks that Griffith shattered that season had belonged
to Harold 'Red' Grange, who remains one of the most recognizable
names associated with the school even 80 years after he last played.

Illinois capped its 1990 season with a berth in the Hall of Fame
Bowl, held in Tampa, Fla. Mike Pearson, the popular UI sports information director, thought it would be good public relations to set up a
meeting between Griffith and Grange, who was living in a retirement
center at Lake Wales, Fla., about an hour from where the team was
staying.

"I called Mrs. Grange and told her Howard had heard all of these
stories about Red Grange and this would be a great opportunity for

them to meet, if she felt Red was up to it," Pearson said.

He said Margaret Grange was receptive in theory, but that her husband had been admitted to a hospital's intensive care unit and she didn't know if the plan would be feasible.

"I discarded the idea altogether," Pearson said.

Two weeks before the Illini left for the New Year's Day game, Pearson received a follow-up call from Mrs. Grange, who wanted to schedule the meeting.

"Howard was thrilled to know it would happen, that he would meet this legendary figure," Pearson said.

Griffith couldn't avoid hearing about the Galloping Ghost, as Grange was called. The 1990 season was the centennial season for football on the UI campus and the school's logo showed Grange running through the columns that grace Memorial Stadium.

The meeting day arrived and Pearson escorted Griffith into the hospital room and made a brief introduction.

"I said, 'Mr. Grange, it's good to see you. I wanted to let you meet the guy who has been breaking all of your records.' " Pearson recalled.

His words were followed by 10 to 15 seconds of silence and Pearson began to have misgivings about the meeting.

"I was thinking, 'He doesn't hear me,' and then a feeble voice says, 'Oh, I know who Howard is,' " Pearson said. "I looked at Howard, and he had this huge grin on his face."

Griffith wasn't the only person who enjoyed the brief meeting.

"That was one of the highlights of my career," Pearson said, "being able to get these two legendary guys together, uniting two stars, one from the present and one from the past. That was one of those special moments."

Grange, who scored four touchdowns in one quarter of a 1924 game against Michigan, died Jan. 28, 1991, of pneumonia. He was 87.

Sheppard was not at the 1990 meeting between Grange and Griffith, but he was part of a ceremony in 1994 that commemorated the 70th anniversary of Grange's game against Michigan.

Margaret Grange was honored in a pregame ceremony at the 1994 Illinois-Michigan contest.

The game marked one of the few times when Sheppard edited the copy he was given to read over the P.A.

Red Grange jersey in the Illinois locker room.

"One of the oldest campustown businesses at the University of Illinois is Campus Florist, owned by Anne Johnston," Sheppard said. "Anne and her late husband, Seely, were longtime friends of Red Grange and his wife, Margaret.

"Red and Seely were college buddies while at Illinois and, for many years, the Johnstons would visit the Granges in Florida. During the week leading up to the (1994) game, I saw Anne and mentioned the announcement I was going to read as the Johnstons were presenting a bouquet of roses to Margaret Grange.

"Anne told me she did not want to be introduced as Mrs. Seely Johnston, but as Anne Johnston. I changed the copy."

Sheppard's announcement:

"Ladies and gentlemen, we direct your attention to the west sideline. We are pleased to have with us Margaret Grange, widow of the greatest player to have ever graced Memorial Stadium. She is being presented a bouquet of roses by Anne and Seely Johnston, longtime friends of the Granges.

"Seventy years ago, in this facility, Illinois and Michigan faced each other in the dedication game of Memorial Stadium. The Illini faced a Michigan team which was unbeaten in its last 20 games, and Illinois featured a junior halfback from Wheaton, Ill., who wore No. 77: Harold 'Red' Grange.

"On the opening play of the game, Grange took Michigan's kickoff at the 5-yard line near the north end zone and ran 95 yards for a touchdown. In the first 12 minutes of the game, he scored the first four times he touched the ball. By game's end, Grange had almost single-handedly beaten Michigan, 39-14.

"In commemoration of the 70th anniversary of this historic event, the University of Illinois has placed a lasting tribute to Red Grange at the north end of Zuppke Field in the form of a 39,000-pound slab of limestone. This limestone comes from the same quarry that supplied the original stonework that was used in constructing Memorial Stadium.

"Ladies and gentlemen, please join in welcoming the wife of the greatest player who ever lived, Mrs. Red Grange."

Illinois put up a valiant effort against the Wolverines the afternoon of the dedication, but lost a 19-14 decision.

Jim standing by the busts of Dick Butkus, left, and Red Grange at the NFL Hall of Fame in Canton, Ohio.

JIM SHEPPARD'S FAVORITE BANDS OR MUSICIANS:

JAZZ
Bob James	His funky keyboard style is great.
Brian Culbertson	He has a unique sound I really enjoy.
Earl Klugh	He ranks right up there with George Benson.

COUNTRY
George Strait	Everything he sings is good.
Earl Thomas Conley	He had some great hits in the '70s and '80s.
Patsy Cline	She had the purest female country voice ever.

ROCK
ZZ Top	I just like the way they rock.
Santana	Their early hits are classics and are still good today.

BLUES
B.B. King	I've seen him twice in person. Nobody does it like B.B.

JIM SHEPPARD'S FAVORITE PROFESSIONAL SPORTS TEAMS:

1) Chicago Cubs. I became hooked early in life. Ernie Banks (Mr. Cub) was my favorite player.
2) New York Yankees. Their history and success are unmatched. My aunt, Velda Kattner, saw Don Larsen's perfect game.
3) Chicago Bears. I can still remember Red Grange and George Conner doing TV games in the 1950s.
4) Indianapolis Colts. I lived in Indy when the team moved from Baltimore.
5) Utah Jazz. I have family who live in Salt Lake City and are fans. The presence of Dee Brown and Deron Williams are reasons, too.

ARE YOU READY?

71

JIM SHEPPARD'S MOST MEMORABLE ILLINI BASKETBALL GAMES FOR YEARS HE ANNOUNCED:

1) Dec. 9, 2000: Vs. Seton Hall. Illini play flat in the first half and trail 42-25 at the break. Coach Bill Self lashes out at guard Frank Williams in the locker room and that's all it took. Williams scores 17 points in the second half and Illinois stages the greatest comeback in school history, resulting in an 87-79 overtime victory. In the OT, Cory Bradford — who sat on the bench the final 5 minutes of regulation — drilled a three-pointer, his first of the game, to tie the NCAA record for consecutive games with a three-pointer (73). Bradford wound up with a still-standing record of 88 straight games making a three-pointer.

2) Feb. 6, 2001: Vs. Michigan State. It was the No. 4 Spartans vs. the No. 7 Illini. If the Illini wanted to win the Big Ten championship that year, they had to take care of the three-time defending champions from East Lansing, Mich. Dick Vitale was in town for the nationally televised game, but it was still a ticket scalper's paradise. There was solid orange everywhere in the Hall. Cory Bradford connected on six three-pointers and the Illini won 77-66 in one of the most exciting games ever at the Assembly Hall.

3) Dec. 1, 2004: Vs. Wake Forest. The visitors were ranked No. 1 but didn't impress the Illini. Illinois dominated the game and won 91-73. The Demon Deacons shot only 39 percent from the field against a solid Illini defense. Roger Powell Jr. led a balanced scoring attack with 19 points.

4) Feb. 4, 1993: Vs. Iowa. Andy Kaufmann catches an inbound pass from T.J. Wheeler with 1.5 seconds remaining and buries a three-pointer to beat the Hawkeyes 78-77. The Assembly Hall crowd explodes.

5) Jan. 22, 1989: Vs. Georgia Tech. The Illini remain undefeated with their 17th consecutive win, a 103-92 decision. The victory lifts Illinois to No. 1 in the country. Kendall Gill suffers a foot injury after scoring 19 points and misses the next 12 games.

6) Feb. 13, 2001: vs. Wisconsin. With 2.5 seconds to play and the Badgers holding a one-point lead, the Illini's 16-game home winning streak, their Big Ten title hopes and a chance for a No. 1 NCAA tournament seed were all on the line. Illinois had the ball on its own baseline and Sean Harrington's inbound pass went to Marcus Griffin, who was under the basket and dropped the ball in with 0.8 second left on the clock. The Badgers threw a long pass the length of the court, which was intercepted by Frank Williams, and that was it. The Illini won 68-67.

7) Feb. 21, 2007: Vs. Michigan. My last game as the public address announcer at the Assembly Hall after 22 years. Dan Maloney as Chief Illiniwek performs for the final time, ending a remarkable 80-year tradition. I'll never forget his surprise encore. Seniors Warren Carter, Rich McBride and Marcus Arnold say goodbye. There was a happy ending as Illinois won 54-42.

8) March 1, 1987: Vs. Indiana. Seniors Ken Norman, Doug Altenberger and Tony Wysinger score 24, 22 and 10 points, respectively, to lead the Illini to a 69-67 win against the No. 3 Hoosiers. Indiana does not lose another game that season and captures the national championship, coach Bob Knight's third and last.

JIM SHEPPARD'S MOST MEMORABLE ILLINI BASKETBALL GAMES FOR YEARS HE ANNOUNCED (CONTINUED):

9) Jan. 28, 1991: Vs. Iowa. Illini legend Harold 'Red' Grange dies early in the day in Florida, the Middle East war continues and I announce for a moment of silence to remember our troops before tipoff. Uniformed police are positioned behind the Iowa bench and the tense feelings continue in the wake of the Deon Thomas-Bruce Pearl recruiting scandal. The Illini win 53-50.

10) Feb. 12, 1998. Vs. Michigan State. The Illini crush the Spartans 84-63 to move coach Lon Kruger's squad into a first-place tie for the Big Ten lead. Michigan State star Mateen Cleaves, who scored 27 points against Illinois earlier, was held to 11 points. The Illini finish the season tied for first in the conference, the first time they tasted a championship since the 1983-84 season.

11) Dec. 11, 1993: Vs. American University. Deon Thomas hits a first-half basket to break Eddie Johnson's career scoring record as the Illini prevail 108-84. Thomas' career total of 2,129 points still ranks first entering the 2007-08 season. After the game, I had a picture taken with Deon. He later autographed it and thanked me for calling out his "three." Thomas made 1 of 2 three-point attempts during his four-year career.

12) March 4, 1990: Vs. Iowa. It was the first game between the two rivals at the Assembly Hall since the NCAA started investigating Illinois' recruitment of Deon Thomas. Illini fans were angry and there was tension in the air. Iowa coach Tom Davis kept assistant coach Bruce Pearl back home. The charged-up Illini rolled to a 118-85 win. Kendall Gill led the way with 25 points.

13) Feb. 12, 2005: Vs. Wisconsin. With 5:34 remaining in the first half, the Badgers' Alando Tucker was called for a foul. I said into the microphone, "That's the first foul on Tucker and only the third foul on Wisconsin." The word "only" was a verbal slip with no harm intended, but it sure caused a stir. I heard later that Wisconsin coach Bo Ryan was upset and said something to the officials at halftime. No one said anything to me after the game, and I forgot about the slip even though I was sorry for my error. Illinois beat Wisconsin 70-59 as an Assembly Hall-record crowd of 16,865 attended.

14) March 9, 1996: Vs. Minnesota. The Illini drop a 67-66 decision to the Golden Gophers in Lou Henson's last regular season game as coach. A tribute program honoring Lou and his wife, Mary, took place after the game on the Assembly Hall court. Henson's final Illini game came four days later, also at the Assembly Hall, a 72-69 loss to Alabama in the NIT.

15) Dec. 22, 1990: Vs. Louisiana State University. After setting a school record by scoring 127 points against the Tigers two years earlier, the Illini beat LSU again, 102-96. The play I remember was Illini guard Rennie Clemons driving down the lane, soaring over Shaquille O'Neal for the basket and forcing Shaq to pick up his fifth personal foul.

Jim says that as a baby he did not miss too many meals.

JIM SHEPPARD'S FAVORITE CHAMPAIGN-URBANA RESTAURANTS, ALL WITH TASTY FOOD:
(listed alphabetically)

Biaggi's Ristorante Italiano	Nice atmosphere and a classy décor.
Chevy's Fresh Mex	Best salsa sauce around.
El Toro	Super fast service.
Jim Gould's	Alive, big-city feel.
Kennedy's at Stone Creek	Relaxing environment with beautiful outside view.
Minneci's	A cozy place, and the table-side chats with owner Joe are always enjoyable.
Original Pancake House	Popular spot with hearty portions.
Philo Tavern	Not in C-U, but close enough.
Silvercreek	Rustic surroundings and unique menu selections.
The Ribeye	The best salad bar in town and great Illini pictures on the walls.

CHAPTER 16

Sheppard has enjoyed the chance to watch some of the nation's all-time basketball coaching greats from his floor-level seat. He had an unforgettable experience with Indiana University head coach Bob Knight, who in January 2007 became the NCAA's winningest coach. Knight is now at Texas Tech.

Prior to announcing the starting lineups when Knight's Indiana team played at the Assembly Hall on Jan. 16, 1993, Sheppard read this tribute:

"Ladies and gentlemen, may I have your attention, please. Yesterday, college basketball lost one of its most respected coaches when the legendary Henry Iba passed away. Iba coached from 1930 to 1970 at Northwest Missouri State, Colorado and for 35 seasons at Oklahoma State University. During his career, he amassed 767 wins to place him second on the all-time list for collegiate coaching victories. At this time, we ask that all present participate in a moment of silence in honor of Coach Iba. Thank you."

After a brief pause, Sheppard did the customary player introductions for both teams.

When he finished, he said, "I raised my head from my script and saw Knight walking toward my position at the scorer's table, glancing my way. My first thought was I had made a mistake regarding the Indiana starters. Knight, who stands 6-foot-4, stood directly in front of me, extended his hand, looked me in the eye, and said very sincerely, 'Thank you for remembering Coach Iba.' I said, 'You're welcome,' and back to the bench Knight went.

"The game was televised and my friends back in Indianapolis watched the incident. The next day, they asked why Knight had come over to me before tipoff."

Indiana won the game 83-79 despite 23 points from Deon Thomas and 14 from Richard Keene.

That was the one and only time that Sheppard and Knight spoke.

Jim poses with Deon Thomas after the forward broke the school record for career points against American University on Dec. 11, 1993.

Sheppard considered much of Knight's conduct to be boorish but respected the job he did as a coach.

"Overall, I thought most of his behavior was unprofessional," Sheppard said, "but if you can overlook that side of Knight and recognize all the positive things he has done, the scale becomes balanced."

Sheppard recalls one time in the early 2000s when the opposing coach was truly less than ecstatic with his performance. The incident occurred during a visit from coach Steve Alford's Iowa Hawkeyes.

"I was introducing the starters and was alternating between each school," Sheppard said, "one from Iowa, one from Illinois and so on. I heard a loud voice yelling at me.

"Alford was complaining that I didn't introduce all five of his starters first, then the five Illinois starters."

It is now a Big Ten Conference rule that the lineups be alternated from one school to the other. At the time, home schools had the option to handle introductions in whatever manner they deemed appropriate.

```
LADIES AND GENTLEMEN ...

WITH THAT BASKET / FREE THROW, DEON THOMAS HAS SCORED THE

1,693rd / 1,694th POINT OF HIS ILLINI CAREER, BREAKING THE RECORD

SET 12 YEARS AGO BY EDDIE JOHNSON.   JOINING DEON AND COACH LOU HENSON

AT CENTER COURT IS DEON'S GRANDMOTHER, BERNICE McGARY.

LET'S HEAR IT FOR THE UNIVERSITY OF ILLINOIS' NEW CAREER SCORING

LEADER, NUMBER 25, DEON THOMAS!
```
Remember tonight Illini fans - because you were a part of Fighting Illini basketball history.
```
Jim:  Deon started tonight's game with 1,672 points.  Eddie Johnson's
      record is 1,692 points.

      Don't announce anything until he surpasses 1,692 points.
```

A copy of the script that was used when
Deon Thomas set the career scoring record.

After the 2007 season, Alford resigned at Iowa to take the head coaching position at New Mexico.

"Oh well," Sheppard said, "no more Steve Alford to deal with."

Jim takes a moment on the field with Illinois centers
Luke Butkus, left, and stepson Brian Scott in 1999.

CHAPTER 17

Unlike newspaper and magazine writers, who often have hours and sometimes days after a game ends to make deadlines, announcers have only a split second to make decisions on what to say or not say.

Sheppard faced one of those moments on Sept. 4, 1999, in the second quarter of Illinois' season opener against Arkansas State.

"The situation happened very quickly," Sheppard said. "Suddenly, starting center Luke Butkus was being assisted off the field and my stepson was quickly practicing a few snaps on the sidelines.

"I normally do not announce substitutions because of an injury unless it's at quarterback. This was a little different because everyone saw Butkus coming off the field, so I said, 'Replacing Luke Butkus, No. 76 Brian Scott.' "

Scott entered with 11:37 remaining in the second quarter and played the remainder of the game, which Illinois won 41-3. He also played in

Jim's in-laws, Lucille and Bill Carlyle with grandson Brian Scott.

three other games that season, including the victory against Virginia in the Micronpc.com Bowl in Miami.

His appearance in the Arkansas State game was a significant moment for his family members. Scott was a senior who made his varsity debut that day.

"My decision to announce Brian's name was based on the injury situation and I did not receive any reaction," Sheppard said. "I was very proud of that moment because Brian always had a never-quit attitude and had contributed to the squad without ever playing.

"His line coach, Harry Hiestand (who went from Illinois to a job with the Chicago Bears) had always told Brian, 'You're just one play away from getting in, so be prepared.' Brian's moment came quickly, and he was prepared."

For the majority of the day's spectators, the announcement of the substitution was no big deal.

"To everyone except my wife, Joan, myself and Brian's grandparents, Bill and Lucille Carlyle, it was nothing special," Sheppard said, "but after being on the team for three years without ever playing a down, the moment was special for us."

Ron Turner, the UI football head coach at the time, did not hear the actual announcement about Scott entering the game.

"I was concentrating on what was happening on the field," Turner said. "I didn't focus too much on the other stuff."

Upon hearing the story, Turner had no problem with Sheppard's decision.

"I said, 'I don't blame you,' " Turner said. "Brian was a great kid who worked hard and didn't get to play a whole lot, but was very valuable. I knew they were proud of Brian."

Sheppard's stepson indirectly influenced another announcing decision Sheppard made. As a senior, Scott shared a house with two Illini teammates, defensive lineman Seth Tesdall, from Morris, and Nathan Hodel, from Fairview Heights.

Sheppard and his wife, Joan, met Tesdall and Hodel as well as their families.

"I mentioned to Nathan one day that the only time fans remember a long-snapper is when they mess up and a field goal or extra point is missed," Sheppard said. "I started announcing the snapper and holder on kick situations for the Illini and the opposing team and still do to this day."

Hodel entered the 2007 football season as the long-snapper for the Arizona Cardinals in the National Football League.

During a 1999 football game against San Diego State, Sheppard showed he was alert to changes at the long-snapper position.

"Hodel had to leave the game early in the second half because of cramps," Sheppard said. "His backup was Champaign Centennial redshirt sophomore Patrick Rouse, who took the field for the first time in his career."

After the 38-10 Illini victory, Rouse said he was hoping the change wouldn't be overlooked.

"Rouse indicated that he anticipated me seeing the change at the snapper position, but didn't know," Sheppard said. "He said that since he was a boy, he dreamed of hearing me announce his name at Memorial Stadium.

"He was afraid I would say, 'Nathan Hodel on the snap.'

"I didn't, and he was pleased."

Sheppard rarely missed a basketball home game — between 1993 and 2007, he was away for just two games — but he can thank his stepson for not attending the Jan. 12, 2002, contest against Michigan. Brian and the former Stacey Foley were married that day.

JIM SHEPPARD'S FAVORITE VACATION SPOTS HE'D LIKE TO VISIT:

1) New England States. I want to visit in the fall to enjoy the colors.
2) Rome. I've been there, but would like to return. A fascinating place and I didn't see all I wanted!
3) Switzerland. A warm fireplace high in the mountains. Wow!
4) London. I'd like to experience the people and history.
5) Rio de Janeiro. I'm fascinated by what I've heard: the music, the excitement, the people.

Jim fishing in the Atlantic Ocean.
Don't ask him how many he caught.

CHAPTER 18

Despite the high points, Sheppard has had a faux pas or two along the way.

"I've always been my own worst critic," he said. "I may notice a minor slip which may not be noticeable to others. There have certainly been games where everything in my announcing has gone smoother than other games."

Throughout his tenure at Illinois, Sheppard has been joined in the Memorial Stadium booth by "loyal and dependable spotters."

A spotter is the person who sits beside the P.A. announcer, usually with binoculars or field glasses, and provides the uniform number of the player making a tackle, carrying the ball or scoring a touchdown.

The moment Sheppard would like most to forget in football took place on Oct. 5, 1985, when the Illini were facing fifth-ranked Ohio State. He still recalls one particular play as if it happened yesterday.

JIM SHEPPARD'S ALL-ILLINI OUT-OF-STATE FOOTBALL TEAM:

(listed alphabetically)

PLAYER	POS.	YEARS	HOMETOWN/HIGH SCHOOL
Mike Bass	K	1980-82	Tampa (Largo), Fla.
Darrick Brownlow	LB	1987-90	Indianapolis (Cathedral)
J.C. Caroline	HB	1953-54	Columbia (Booker T. Washington), S.C.
Ralph Chapman	OG	1912-14	Washington (Central), D.C.
Jason Dulick	WR	1993-96	St. Louis (University High)
Tony Eason	QB	1981-82	Walnut Grove (Delta), Calif.
Moe Gardner	NT	1987-90	Indianapolis (Cathedral)
Mike Gow	DB	1972-74	Farmington (North), Mich.
Kevin Hardy	LB	1992-95	Evansville (Harrison), Ind.
Robert Holcombe	RB	1994-97	Mesa, Ariz.
Brandon Lloyd	WR	1999, 2001-02	Blue Springs, Mo.
Bobby Mitchell	HB	1955-57	Hot Springs (Langston), Ark.
Chris Richardson	K	1991-94	Richardson (Berkner), Texas
Scott Studwell	LB	1973-76	Evansville (Harrison), Ind.
Archie Sutton	OT	1962-64	New Orleans (Savier), La.
Al Tate	OT	1948-50	New Castle, Pa.
Jack Trudeau	QB	1983-85	Livermore (Granada), Calif.
Jason Verduzco	QB	1989-92	Antioch, Calif.
David Williams	WR	1983-85	Los Angeles (Serra), Calif.
Eugene Wilson	DB	1999-2002	Merrillville, Ind.

JIM SHEPPARD'S ALL-ILLINI OUT-OF-STATE BASKETBALL TEAM:

(listed alphabetically)

PLAYER	POS.	YEARS	HOMETOWN/HIGH SCHOOL
Rich Adams	F	1975-78	Cincinnati (Colerain)
Cory Bradford	G	1999-2002	Memphis (Raleigh Egypt), Tenn.
Tal Brody	G	1963-65	Trenton (Central), N.J.
Bill Burwell	C	1961-63	Brooklyn (Boys), N.Y.
James Griffin	C	1979-82	Grandview (Dunbar), Texas
Derek Harper	G	1981-83	West Palm Beach (North Shore), Fla.
Mike Price	G	1968-70	Indianapolis (Arsenal Tech)
Nick Weatherspoon	F	1971-73	Canton (McKinley), Ohio
Anthony Welch	F	1982-83, 1985-86	Grand Rapids (Creston), Mich.
Deron Williams	G	2003-05	The Colony (High), Texas

"Late in the game, quarterback Jack Trudeau connected on a long pass down the east sidelines with receiver Stephen Pierce, who wore No. 7," Sheppard said. "As Pierce got up after his circus catch, he had his arm across the top of the seven, so it looked like the number '1.' "

For Sheppard, the spotter with the most longevity is his good friend, Rich Piccioli, who provided the information that the reception on the play that covered almost 40 yards against the Buckeyes was made by David Williams, who wore No. 1. Sheppard made the announcement, and the game continued.

"A few seconds later, Tab Bennett, the Illinois Sports Information Director, rushed into our booth and told me it was not Williams who made the reception. It was Pierce," Sheppard said. "As Pierce went back to the sidelines, his Illini teammates told him that I announced Williams' name instead.

"Both Piccioli and I felt bad, but it certainly was an explainable mistake. The next week, Piccioli phoned Pierce and apologized."

Pierce wasn't totally overlooked that day. He caught seven passes for 131 yards as the Illini won 31-28.

Pierce, who now lives in San Diego, took the announcement in stride.

"It never bothered me," he said. "I knew I could play. It's all good as long as we win."

Pierce said he never actually heard what Sheppard said at the time.

"When I step on the field, I don't hear the crowd or see the people," Pierce said. "It's like I'm at home."

Having the two talented receivers on the same team didn't affect their relationship. They harbored no animosity toward each other.

"Dave is one of my best friends," Pierce said. "We plan our trips to come to Champaign together."

As for Sheppard's work, Pierce heard enough at different times to

Jim on the field with stepson Brian Scott, left,
and current NFL linebacker Danny Clark.

Jim stands between ABC-TV announcer Gary Bender, left,
and Pittsburgh Steeler Hall of Famer Lynn Swann.

form a favorable opinion.

"He's one of the greatest and I respected him," Pierce said.

Piccioli said the incident involving Pierce is one he and Sheppard can look back on now and smile about.

"There were 76,000 people in the stands and the only two who didn't know who made the catch were the P.A. and his offensive spotter," Piccioli said. "We have a running joke now, 'This is a '1.' This is a '7.' "

Whether it's a major gaffe or a minor slip-up, Sheppard feels badly when a mistake occurs.

Working with defensive spotter John Truscelli, from Rantoul, at another football game, Sheppard caught a potential error before he spoke.

"John was dependable showing up for the games at Memorial Stadium, but at times I had to remind him to stay focused on giving me the tacklers on plays," Sheppard said.

"John's wife Debbie would attend games and sit in the east balcony on many occasions. John would sometimes be watching Debbie with his binoculars right before the ball was snapped. During a game many seasons ago, I noticed out of the corner of my eye that John was looking towards the east balcony right before a play."

A running play was called and Sheppard waited the customary few seconds to hear the number of the tackler. When Truscelli said nothing, Sheppard questioned him.

"I asked, 'John, do you have a number for me?' " Sheppard said. "John responded with some uncertainty in his voice, 'Uh, No. 50.' I could not believe I heard John say 'No. 50.'

"I turned to him and said, 'Come on, John. Get in the game. No. 50 is hanging in the Illini locker room. It belonged to Dick Butkus and that number is retired.' "

That incident led to a positive change. Sheppard said, "Truscelli paid more attention to details after that."

Piccioli estimated that there are about 170 plays per game. Sometimes by the time the final few are attempted, there are some strange comments in the P.A. booth.

"One time, the team had the ball on the 48 and moved it across midfield," Piccioli said. "I told Jim the ball was on the 52. He just looked at me."

One reason to strive for accuracy is to avoid being remembered for the mistakes that were made.

In a 1985 interview with The Daily Illini, Sheppard said he goes to great lengths to say names correctly, especially if the player is someone who doesn't play much.

"If I was a father coming down for a game and on the only play my son made, his name was said wrong, I would remember it for the rest of my life. I don't want that to happen," Sheppard told the D.I.'s Shezad Bandukwala.

Sheppard had not even joined the UI team when his first embarrassing moment happened.

He was employed at WDWS and one of his perks was to gain access to the station's broadcasting booth on game day. He enjoyed watching the game from that perch.

"On one particular day, Claude 'Buddy' Young from the 1940s was in the booth before he was to go down to the field at halftime to receive an award," Sheppard said. "I had just been introduced to Buddy and felt good to be in the presence of a former All-American.

"The booth was rather crowded that game and I was sipping on a cup of orange soda. Someone accidentally bumped my arm and my beverage spilled all over Mr. Young's shirt and tie. You can imagine how low I felt."

Young graciously took the incident in stride.

"I'll never forget what Buddy said to me," Sheppard added. " 'Don't worry young man, I'll simply button my coat and no one will see.' "

Another press box incident that could have turned into something major, did not.

"A few years ago, the Illini hosted Minnesota," Sheppard said. "During the first half, I consumed more water than usual. As the second quarter wound down, I was feeling an urgent need to visit the men's bathroom as soon as the half ended.

"I was already standing as the last play was about to unfold so I could exit the booth ASAP. With just a few seconds remaining, Minnesota called a needless timeout. I gritted my teeth even harder."

When the half ended, Sheppard said, "out the booth I flew."

JIM SHEPPARD'S FIVE PEOPLE HE'D LIKE TO HAVE DINNER WITH:

1) My grandparents Sheppard: They both passed away before I was born.
2) Actor Anthony Hopkins: I've enjoyed all of his performances.
3) Comedian Jonathan Winters: He's an interesting man. Maudie Frickert character and dessert would be a blast.
4) Bob Sheppard: The longtime P.A. voice of the New York Yankees, now in his 90s. The stories would be terrific. (No relation to Jim.)
5) Actress Sophia Loren: She is a beautiful star who has led a fascinating life.

Jim enjoying his Christmas bike.

Jim on vacation in California. He says flying over
the Pacific coastline was awesome.

JIM SHEPPARD'S YEAR-BY-YEAR FOOTBALL GAMES ANNOUNCED:

1985: 6	1991: 6	1997: 6	2003: 6
1986: 6	1992: 6	1998: 6	2004: 7
1987: 6	1993: 6	1999: 6	2005: 6
1988: 6	1994: 7	2000: 7	2006: 7
1989: 5	1995: 6	2001: 6	
1990: 6	1996: 6	2002: 6	Total: 135

JIM SHEPPARD'S YEAR-BY-YEAR MEN'S BASKETBALL GAMES ANNOUNCED:

1985-86: 17	1993-94: 16	2001-02: 14	NOTE: Jim missed
1986-87: 15	1994-95: 15	2002-03: 16	four home games
1987-88: 16	1995-96: 17	2003-04: 14	while living in In-
1988-89: 17	1996-97: 16	2004-05: 16	dianapolis.
1989-90: 14	1997-98: 15	2005-06: 17	
1990-91: 16	1998-99: 14	2006-07: 18	
1991-92: 16	1999-2000: 14		
1992-93: 16	2000-01: 14	Total: 343	

CHAPTER 19

Words do not always come out the way Sheppard intended. The situation is compounded when the basketball game happens to be on national television.

"Without a doubt, the most embarrassing moment I had happened on Dec. 3, 1994, at the United Center in Chicago," Sheppard said.

The Illini and sixth-ranked Duke were playing the first collegiate game ever in the United Center facility known as "The House that Jordan built."

CBS had Billy Packer and Jim Nance courtside to handle the telecast.

As was his custom, Sheppard arrived early and was going through his pregame checklist when a man from CBS handed him a script to be read at the outset of the telecast.

It read: "Welcome to the United Center for the first-ever college

ARE YOU READY?

91

Jim with Miss Florida Citrus at the 1990 Citrus Bowl in Orlando, Fla. The Illini beat Virginia 31-21.

game between the Fighting Illini from the University of Illinois and the Duke Blue Devils."

The words were not out of the ordinary, nor were they particularly challenging. However, when Sheppard spoke, the whole country heard his blooper.

"I said the Bluke Due Devils," he said, "and inside, I died a thousand deaths. I recovered my composure and got through the starting line-ups."

It wasn't enough that he said it once.

"That night," he said, "a Chicago TV station carried my blunder on their news."

Duke won the game 70-65 despite a game-high 19 points from Kiwane Garris.

Some folks have keen memories. More than a dozen years later, Sheppard said, "people still kid me about the 'Bluke Due Devils.' "

That mistake made a previous basketball mistake seem insignificant.

"In my first season of announcing," Sheppard said, "the opposing team had a starting guard that stood 5-foot-4. When I introduced him, I somehow said '6-foot-4.' As the little guy ran onto the court, he looked back at me with a big smile."

Sometimes, knowing what to say — and saying it precisely right — still causes confusion.

On Oct. 5, 1996, the Illini and Indiana football teams were tied after regulation the first year the Big Ten put rules into effect governing overtimes.

"I knew what the overtime rule was," Sheppard said, "but I did not feel comfortable ad-libbing it to the fans."

Dana Brenner, an athletic administrator from the UI, hurried out of the P.A. booth and returned with a copy of the NCAA Rule Book

Heather Coit/The News-Gazette

Illinois' Dee Brown goes up for a layup against Longwood
on Dec. 27, 2004. The Illini won 105-79.

opened to the section that detailed procedures for overtimes.

"As a lot of things with the NCAA are, the rule book wording was long, complex and rather hard for the fan's ear to digest," Sheppard said. "As I read the long details, I could hear fans laughing from outside our booth window."

With Scott Weaver throwing a 26-yard touchdown pass to Jason Dulick, the Illini secured the win in double overtime, 46-43, with 55,534 spectators watching. By the time the next home game arrived, Sheppard remembers, "needless to say, a short, simple and distinct page was prepared for me."

There was not another overtime game at Memorial Stadium that season.

Sheppard said, "other than a rare technical problem with my headset or my microphone needing an adjustment," nothing strange has ever occurred while the mic was live.

"One incident that I remember happened during my last season at the Assembly Hall," Sheppard said. "As I was reading an announcement at halftime, I felt these two arms around me from behind.

"After a brief hug, they went away. After the announcement, I turned to the person next to me and asked who had come up while I was reading. The person said, 'Dee Brown.'

"I noticed Dee standing at the end of the scorer's table, so I approached him, gave him a hug and said hello. It will always be good to see Dee."

Jim at age 7 in 1955. "I finally gave up thoughts of professional rodeo work and went into sports."

JIM SHEPPARD'S FAVORITE HOBBIES:

1) Producing videos: I've done this for years and find it very rewarding.
2) Traveling: Far-away locations or close to home, I always enjoy going to where I've never been.
3) Collecting sports memorabilia: I've got a good collection and am interested in adding to my Illini items.
4) Spending time with family and friends: Sharing special moments with those you love and care for, and watching my grandchildren grow, is fabulous.
5) Kiwanis Club: I'm actively involved in this international organization and believe in the positive projects we do.

CHAPTER 20

At times, mistakes seem like they're as close as the next sentence.

One of Sheppard's most daunting challenges occurred during Lou Henson's tenure when the preseason opponent was a Russian touring team.

"When I received the roster and looked at the names, I knew I was in trouble," Sheppard said.

He wanted to leave nothing to chance.

"Sports Information Director Tab Bennett put me in touch with a Slavic language professor at the University of Illinois," Sheppard said. "I called him and he invited me to visit him at his office with my list of multi-syllable Russian basketball names.

"As I sat with him in his small, cramped office, the professor spoke the names into a cassette recorder I had taken with me. I took the list and my recorded cassette back home and worked on the pronunciations for about two weeks."

By game day, Sheppard's confidence level was high. "I had the names down pretty well, but without the Russian accent," he said.

As a final precaution, he contacted the SID office at Illinois and spoke with Dick Barnes, "just to be sure the Russian team's roster was what I had been working on."

Sheppard felt like a jilted lover.

"As I started down the list, Dick said, 'He's not here tonight,' and 'That player won't be here.' About half of the names I had been practicing were not going to be at the Assembly Hall," Sheppard said.

He arrived extra early to the Assembly Hall to speak with a representative of the Russian squad.

"This gentleman understood English, but did not speak our language well enough for me to understand," Sheppard said.

By tipoff, Sheppard thought he was as ready as he could be.

"Through the grace of the basketball god, I finally had the new players' correct pronunciations down so I could get through the game," he said.

He expected an 'A' for his effort, but not necessarily for his production. He was surprised by the feedback he received.

"After the contest was finished, the Russian coach approached me and told me I had done the best job of all the P.A. announcers his team had played before," Sheppard said. "His sincere compliment made the weeks of practicing and the late roster changes worthwhile."

One name Sheppard never had trouble with was a tongue-twister for other announcers: Kiwane Garris, a Chicago Westinghouse graduate who played for the Illini from 1993 to '97.

"His first name was different and the correct pronunciation was KEY-wahn, but often it was mispronounced," Sheppard said. "Once at Williams Arena, home of the Minnesota Golden Gophers, Garris was introduced as Ki-Wayne. Other times it was Ki-WAHNEY.

"Garris once said, 'I'm always telling people the "e" is silent, but they don't listen.' "

Garris' name is a prominent one in the UI record books. He ranks as the No. 2 career scorer (1,948 points), No. 1 for career free throws made (615) and first for consecutive free throws made (39). He is the only Illini to hit all 17 free throw attempts in a game, doing so in 1996 against California.

"In my opinion," Sheppard said, "if there was ever an argument about who did not make the Illinois All-Century Basketball Team, but deserved to be on it, I'd start with Kiwane Garris."

Jim with one of his favorite Illini, basketball guard Kiwane Garris.

Jim's graduation ceremony at Fisher High School, walking next to classmate Janet Rappleyea in 1966.

Jim and his little sister Mary Jane at Easter in 1956.

CHAPTER 21

Sheppard has a plethora of memories from Illinois games. Two note-worthy contests took place before he was handling the P.A. duties.

On Nov. 8, 1969, "one of the funniest and memorable one-liners I ever heard in the Memorial Stadium press box occurred," Sheppard said.

The Illini football team, under the direction of coach Jim Valek, brought an 0-7 record into a game with Michigan.

Sheppard was working at WDWS and, though he was not on-air, joined the crew in the Champaign station's broadcasting booth. Leg-endary comedian Bob Hope was in town to perform at the Assembly Hall that night and he also made his way to the booth.

"Hope and former Illini coach Ray Eliot (who was by now part of the UI broadcasting team with Larry Stewart) had developed a friend-ship over the years after meeting in California when Eliot took his

Illinois teams to the Rose Bowl," Sheppard said.

Hope occupied the seat between Stewart and Eliot on an afternoon when the Wolverines were clobbering the Illini.

"The mood in the booth was pretty gloomy," said Sheppard, who remembered the light-hearted moment taking place in the fourth quarter when Michigan defensive back Bruce Elliott intercepted a pass from Illinois' Steve Livas and returned it 40 yards for a touchdown.

"Elliott was a standout player for coach Tommy Stewart's Champaign Central (high school) teams and the son of former Illinois coach Pete Elliott," Sheppard said. "As Elliott ran the interception back, Hope said, 'That looks like Crosby going to the bank,' a reference to fellow comedian Bing Crosby.

"The line brought a laugh to those in the booth, but it was the only chuckle of the day. Michigan won 57-0."

That defeat was the worst for an Illini team since 1906, when the University of Chicago blanked Illinois 63-0.

On Dec. 24, 1983, the Illini played host to Kentucky in basketball. A winter storm made road conditions throughout central Illinois treacherous, and the officials assigned to work the game were stranded on the interstate and unable to make it to Champaign.

"Three area men were called out of the stands, put on the stripes and officiated the game (won by the Wildcats 56-54)," Sheppard said. "They were Monticello High School principal Bill Mitze, University of Illinois professor Bob Hiltibran and Champaign Central High School baseball coach Charlie Due.

"The trio was praised after the game by Illini coach Lou Henson and Kentucky coach Joe B. Hall."

Sheppard and Due had been friends for years and they teamed up when Sheppard became the public address announcer at home Illini football games.

"He was my spotter for my first Illinois football game two years later," Sheppard said. "Unfortunately, I worked with Charlie only one game, my first game against Southern Cal. The next Friday, after officiating a high school football game in Decatur, Charlie Due suffered a heart attack and died.

"He was a good friend."

Jim with Hall of Fame Cardinals
broadcaster Jack Buck, right.

Former Illini and Baseball Hall of Famer Lou Boudreau with Jim.

CHAPTER 22

Sheppard saw his first UI basketball game in person before he was a teenager and before the Assembly Hall was built.

He was at Huff Hall for a contest late in the 1959-60 season, a year in which the Illini finished the season with three straight wins to salvage a tie for third place in the Big Ten.

Sheppard did not see a winner when Indiana provided the opposition on Feb. 22, 1960.

"Star center Walt Bellamy poured in 42 points in the 92-78 Hoosier win," Sheppard said.

Another Indiana game is also prominent in Sheppard's mind. It took place on Jan. 23, 2007.

"Indiana, with new head coach Kelvin Sampson, visited the Assembly Hall," Sheppard said. "Because of the Eric Gordon recruiting issue (the Indiana high schooler who gave an oral commitment to Illinois but later changed his mind), Illini fans exploded into a sea of boos as Sampson emerged from the tunnel before tipoff.

"An Assembly Hall employee who controls the sound levels during the games had told me the loudest he had ever measured was when former Hoosier coach Bob Knight walked out before a game."

Doug Pugh, a stagehand at the UI who has done audio for the basketball home games for 19 years, believes the game was the year after Lou Henson had referred to Knight as a "classic bully."

Said Pugh: "As I recall, the resounding screams and boos hit .105 decibels unassisted, with no band, on the calibrated meter, and I'm in B section."

After the Illini beat Sampson and the Hoosiers 51-43 in the 2007 game, Sheppard was certain that record had been broken.

"It was as loud as it has ever been."

Jim with the greatest all-around athlete in Illini history, Dike Eddleman.

CHAPTER 23

Dwight 'Dike' Eddleman's fabled UI career as the winner of 11 varsity letters had ended before Sheppard was born, but the two men built a friendship while attending the weekly UI football press lunches.

"We always talked about the Illini and I took advantage of my time with Dike by asking about how things were during his Illini days," Sheppard said. "Dike loved to reminisce and I loved to listen."

A few weeks before Eddleman went into the hospital for the final time in 2001, the two men were joined at a table by Charlie Finn, a longtime UI supporter and a friend of Eddleman.

"Dike was noticeably not feeling well but never complained," Sheppard said. "A few minutes into the lunch, the three of us started talking about Dike's playing days.

"The topic turned to the Illinois-Army game played at New York's Yankee Stadium in 1947. The Illini entered the game ranked sixth in the country and Army was fifth.

"Dike's mood brightened up as we talked. He recalled a play where he had the ball and was running toward a touchdown but fumbled the ball because of the perspiration on his hands. Dike said in a determined tone, 'Boy, I wish I had that play back.'"

The Illini-Army contest ended in a 0-0 deadlock.

"Shortly before Dike passed away, I visited him at Carle Foundation Hospital," Sheppard said. "I remember that he didn't talk about himself but asked me how I was doing. I'll never forget that."

Following Eddleman's death, Sheppard was chosen as an honorary pallbearer.

"I cried," Sheppard said. "I was so humbled that they had given me this honor. As anyone who ever knew him will remember, besides his legendary athletic accomplishments, Dike was an even better person."

As a youth, Sheppard was able to watch the exploits of another all-time Illini great, fullback Jim Grabowski. They later met in a professional capacity when Grabowski served as color commentator for the WDWS game broadcasts.

"When I was in school, high school students could sit in the Memorial Stadium horseshoe for $1," Sheppard said. "What a bargain in those days to see such Illini players as Grabowski, Dick Butkus, Don Hansen, George Donnelly, Archie Sutton and others for only a buck.

"I enjoyed watching the rugged Grabowski play. He was the most prolific three-year runner in Illinois history. The three runners ahead of him (Robert Holcombe, Antoineo Harris and Thomas Rooks) each had four seasons to get their yards."

Sheppard said when he subsequently met Grabowski, "he always was friendly and cordial."

CHAPTER 24

Illinois' 1988-89 basketball team, which reached the NCAA Final Four, was dubbed the Flyin' Illini for its fast-paced style and tremendous leaping ability.

Sheppard was an example of the "flying" theme himself during that marathon run.

"I lived in Indianapolis and worked in radio that season," Sheppard said, "but drove back to Champaign on game days to announce."

Coach Lou Henson's squad won its first 17 games.

"Win No. 17 was a double-overtime victory on a Sunday afternoon against Georgia Tech at the Assembly Hall," Sheppard said. "It propelled Illinois to No. 1 in the country.

"Unfortunately, Kendall Gill was injured in the Georgia Tech game and the Illini lost their first game of the season the following week at Minnesota."

The Big Ten's second-place team started NCAA tournament play in Indianapolis, a short commute for the announcer who was able to enjoy the action as a spectator.

A week later, he was glued to his television set watching the Illini dispatch Syracuse in Minneapolis to qualify for the Final Four in Seattle, where the team's championship hopes were dashed in the semifinals by Michigan.

During the seven years Sheppard lived and worked in Indianapolis, inclement winter conditions never prevented him from traveling to UI home games.

"I was extremely fortunate that I never missed a game as a result of bad weather or car problems," he said. "I do recall an eight-day period during the basketball season when the Illini played three home games.

"Interstate 74 was hazardous, the temperatures were very cold and I was physically whipped after working all day and traveling four hours roundtrip and announcing the game.

"When I walked out of the Assembly Hall shortly after 9 o'clock Champaign time, it was an hour later in Indianapolis. The good Lord was with me during those years."

While living the life of the long-distance commuter, Sheppard developed a regular routine on game day.

"My time schedule was tight on weekday basketball games," Sheppard said. "I would leave work in Indy at 5 o'clock (EST), planning on a comfortable two-hour drive.

"By the time I arrived at the northeast Assembly Hall parking lot, it was approximately one hour before tipoff, providing it was a 7 o'clock game (CST)."

Once he relocated back to the Champaign-Urbana area, Sheppard said, "I was always in the Assembly Hall two hours before the game's start."

CHAPTER 25

By the time Illinois made another run to the Final Four, during the 2004-05 season, Sheppard was living in Champaign County.

It's impossible, he said, to select one favorite memory from that season.

"So many things run through my mind," he said, "the buzz here in Champaign-Urbana, how the entire state rallied around the team, the dominance over No. 1 Wake Forest (91-73 at the Assembly Hall on Dec. 1, 2004), a win which helped move the Illini up to No. 1 in the country after another game, and the same five starters all season long (each of whom averaged in double figures), the terrific trio of guards, Luther Head, Dee Brown and Deron Williams along with Roger Powell Jr. and James Augustine.

"I remember how most everyone thought the Illini could be really good that season, but no one knew it would turn into the greatest season in school history."

The season started with successive blowouts of Delaware State (20 points), Florida A&M (31 points) and Oakland (also 31 points).

Even the Adam Morrison-led Gonzaga squad proved to be no match. In the John Wooden Tradition game at Conseco Fieldhouse in Indianapolis, the Illini led 58-27 at halftime and cruised to an 89-72 victory.

"The stage was set for the showdown with top-ranked Wake Forest at the Assembly Hall, and I recall the atmosphere was as electric as it has ever been," Sheppard said.

With four of five Illini starters scoring in double figures, coach Bruce Weber's team raced to leads as large as 32 points in the second half before settling for an 18-point conquest.

"Their two highly-touted stars, Chris Paul and Justin Gray, were never a factor," Sheppard said. "The Illini were unstoppable. I knew this was the start of something very special for that season."

Another highlight game for Sheppard took place on Jan. 29, 2005. The Illini routed Minnesota 89-66 for their 21st consecutive win. Long after folks had forgotten that Powell was the game's top scorer (21 points) or that Williams made as many three-pointers as the Gophers (four) in nine fewer attempts, the circumstances of that Saturday game will keep it a prominent part of the season.

In conjunction with Illinois' 100-year celebration of basketball, dozens of former players returned.

"The first Illini team I identified with as a kid was the 1958-59 team featuring Govoner Vaughn, Mannie Jackson and Johnny Wessels," said Sheppard, who was an impressionable 11-year-old at the time.

I told myself if I could meet just one person during the Centennial Celebration weekend, it would be Govoner Vaughn. I thought he had the coolest name and I always liked how he played."

Fate was kind to Sheppard that week during a special luncheon.

"Govoner entered the room and I immediately noticed him," Sheppard said. "I had never met him, but when I saw him it brought back memories from my childhood. I approached him and introduced myself. He was very soft-spoken and gracious. I told him he was my favorite Illini growing up."

As Illinois' magical season continued, Sheppard was at the heart of another special moment just two weeks after meeting Vaughn.

With a minute left in a Feb. 12, 2005, game against Wisconsin (which the Illini won 70-59), Sheppard made this announcement: "You were a part of Illini basketball history today — the largest crowd in Assembly Hall history, 16,865."

Illinois won its first 29 games during the 2004-05 season before suffering a one-point loss at Ohio State. The team then won eight more games to advance into the national championship game.

"Just being a part of the home games that season is something I'll always cherish," said Sheppard, who joined his good friend Charlie Finn in St. Louis for the April 4 NCAA title game, when North Carolina posted a 75-70 win.

Jim meets with, from left, good friend Charlie Finn and former Illini football stars J.C. Caroline and John Wright Sr.

Jerrance Howard carries the trophy into the hangar at FlightStar. Deron Williams is behind Howard. Fans greeted the team on its homecoming March 7, 2004, after the Illini won the Big Ten Conference regular season championship at Ohio State 64-63.

CHAPTER 26

Jerrance Howard, a Peoria native, was on a recruiting visit to Illinois when he noticed more than the atmosphere at the Assembly Hall.

"I noticed Sheppard's voice when I went to my first Illini game against Michigan," Howard said. "His voice always stood out."

That wasn't all, said Howard.

"He had one of the biggest smiles in the Assembly Hall," Howard said. "He never had a bad day. He was a first-class guy, just one of my favorites."

Howard eventually played for the Illini from 2000 to '04 and then entered the coaching profession. In April 2007, he was hired as an assistant at the University of Kentucky.

Both as a player and as a coach, Howard has had the chance to observe various public address announcers. Sheppard is at the top of his list.

Jim at the microphone in the Assembly Hall, waiting for the next call.

"No disrespect to anyone else," Howard said, "but it doesn't even come close. He had a passion and definitely separated himself.

"It always started with Jim at the Assembly Hall. He set the whole tone from the time we came on the floor until the time we left. He is one of the reasons we had a homecourt advantage. It's hard to imagine the Assembly Hall without Jim. He has been loyal to the program."

Howard had a ritual he followed prior to every home game.

"I used to go down and shake his hand," Howard said. "That's one memory I won't forget."

By the time Howard enrolled at school, former staff member Mark Coomes was an assistant coach at Illinois-Chicago. The time away didn't diminish Coomes' respect and admiration for Sheppard.

"He had a classy way of announcing," Coomes said. "Jim did exactly what the game's management people wanted. He was not a homer, but was professional and classy, sort of down the middle.

"For that, he gets a big A-plus."

Coomes remembers that when he joined Lou Henson's coaching staff in the mid-1970s, the student pep band had no similarity to what it is today.

"It was more of an orchestral ensemble than hype and noise," Coomes said. "They had a concert band dressed in coats and ties."

The Orange Krush was introduced by Henson, and the aura of the Assembly Hall took off in a wildly popular direction.

"We had a great pep band, we had the Orange Krush, and I was always very appreciative of the work Jim did to market the program," Coomes said.

"Part of that marketing is a voice you can identify. All of those things are part of the atmosphere. There's nobody that stands out better than Jim."

As Illinois basketball became the hot ticket in town, Sheppard reached icon status. Deservedly so, according to Coomes.

"Everything changed and Illinois became one of the toughest venues in the country to play," Coomes said. "Jim had a historic part in how Illinois has evolved from an excitement standpoint."

Robin Scholz/The News-Gazette

UI basketball coach Bruce Weber is always animated on the sidelines — like during this Nov. 18, 2005, game against South Dakota State.

CHAPTER 27

For years, Sheppard had one of the best — and least unobstructed — views of the Illini basketball home games.

"I felt lucky and very fortunate to be sitting where I did at courtside," he said.

His location didn't mean he was involved in pregame banter with coaches or players.

"With what's at stake in college athletics today," Sheppard said, "I hardly see any joking among players and coaches before a game."

For several seasons, Sheppard was seated beside Tony Clements, who took over as the team's official scorer in 1985. Sheppard's first basketball spotter was Stevie Jay, from WDWS.

"He wrote down the substitutions for both teams as they checked into the game," Sheppard said. "I think the most subs we ever had in one game was 98 against Iowa. The Hawkeyes' coach at the time, Tom

A look at Jim's two favorite places to take in a game:
Memorial Stadium, left, and the Assembly Hall.

Davis, would regularly send in three and four players together."

Dave Johnson, from the Division of Intercollegiate Athletics, also served for a time as a spotter, and in Sheppard's final season, 2006-07, his lookout was UI marketing director Chris Hanna.

When you've been around as long as Sheppard, there's a degree of notoriety that comes with the territory.

"Several years ago, I was on a commercial air flight speaking to the person next to me," Sheppard said. "A lady behind me tapped me on the shoulder and asked if I was the person who did the Illini games.

"I told her 'Yes.' Her husband, sitting beside her, had heard my voice and knew who I was, but wanted his wife to confirm it."

A little recognition also occurred during the 2004-05 season.

"I was having lunch one day in Aunt Sonya's," Sheppard said. "A waitress who knew who I was mentioned my name to a Chicago TV news crew who was in town to cover the pep rally at the Assembly Hall before the team headed to the Final Four in St. Louis.

"The crew approached me and wanted to do a short interview with me about being the P.A. announcer for the Illini that season."

Snippets of the conversation were aired on the station that night.

The most common scenario, Sheppard said, is that folks recognize his voice and "start talking Illini sports with me."

It's not difficult to recognize Sheppard if you're driving around the Champaign-Urbana area. His license plates read 'UI ANNCR.'

That wasn't his first choice when he applied for the special plates.

"I requested 'THATS A 3,' but I received a letter back from the Secretary of State's office informing me that plate was already taken," Sheppard said.

"I was really surprised and was later told that former Illini sharp-shooter Richard Keene had it. I never confirmed it, but I do know 'THATS A 3' is not now being used. After receiving the letter from the state, I applied for 'UI ANNCR,' and that's what I have today."

Jim has met plenty of famous TV personalities
over the years, like Keith Jackson, left, and Dick Vitale.

CHAPTER 28

Sheppard has found requests from coaches and players to have been few and far between.

Two noteworthy exceptions came from Lou Henson.

Sheppard's first season behind the microphone was for the 1985-86 season, which coincided with the arrival of junior college transfer Ken Norman, who had the nickname "Snake."

Baskets by Norman were accompanied by more than the mention of his name.

"I started making a hissing noise, like a snake, whenever Norman scored," Sheppard said. "The fans started picking up on the sound because I could hear them. Henson did not like me using the sound and so I was told not to use it anymore."

Later that same season, Michigan State and Big Ten Conference scoring leader Scott Skiles — now the head coach of the Chicago

Bulls — journeyed to Champaign-Urbana.

In addition to putting together a streak of five consecutive 30-point games as a senior, Skiles was dealing with outside issues. He committed a parole violation on an earlier marijuana conviction and served a brief jail sentence.

"A few days before Michigan State played at the Assembly Hall (on Feb. 6, 1986), I ran into Henson," Sheppard said. "Lou was concerned that I didn't say anything extra about Skiles in my announcing the starting lineups that would get our fans riled up.

"I told Lou I only announce a player's height, year in school, hometown and uniform number in my starting lineup. Skiles always got opposing crowds to challenge him and he loved it."

Michigan State beat the Illini 84-80. Skiles, who entered the game ranked second in the nation in scoring (26.9 average), scored 25.

Sheppard remembered one request which was ignored. It came on Nov. 15, 2002, when the Illini played host to EA Sports All-Stars in an exhibition game.

Three former Illini — Lucas Johnson, Sergio McClain and Marcus Griffin — were in uniform for the All-Stars.

"Johnson asked me if I would shout out, 'That's a three ... Lucas Johnson,' if he hit a trey," Sheppard recalled.

Johnson made two of the long-range shots in the game, but didn't get his wish from the P.A. announcer.

"I never said it," Sheppard said. "I liked Lucas and enjoyed his tough style as an Illini, but that night, he was an Illini opponent."

Former Illini head coach Bill Self never found it necessary to make a request to Sheppard.

"I didn't worry too much about the stuff I didn't have control over," Self said. "I like for the introductions to be good, but I've had zero input on how we do things.

"(The P.A. announcers) do a good job and I go with the flow."

Self left the Illini for the head coaching position at Kansas following the 2002-03 season. During the 2006-07 season — when a substitute announcer filled in for the Jayhawks — Self expressed his feelings on something he didn't want to hear repeated.

"We had a player (sophomore Mario Chalmers) score and they said, 'Super Mario,' " Self said. "I said, 'No, we don't do that.' "

As for his stint at Illinois, Self said he was pleased with Sheppard's work.

"You want someone who provides energy through the game and I felt that Jim did that," Self said. "I liked how he called the three-point shots. He put a good twist on the guys who shot the threeball. He did a great job."

Former Illinois football coach Bob Zuppke, third from left, was joined by other UI dignitaries when he was honored in 1949. Ray Eliot, left, and Arthur Hall, second from left, were joined by ex-Illini Lou Boudreau, the Cleveland Indians baseball manager. Eliot was the UI football coach while Hall was a former coach who was running for re-election as Judge of the Probate Court of Vermilion County.

Jim chats it up at a function with former
Illini football greats J.C. Caroline, left, and Abe Woodson.

CHAPTER 29

Though his early childhood hero was J.C. Caroline, Sheppard's connection to and interest in Illinois athletics didn't mushroom until after the 11-year-old attended his first football game.

The opponent for the Oct. 3, 1959, game was Army, the nation's fourth-ranked team. By then, Caroline's collegiate career had ended.

"The Cadets featured a player named Bill Carpenter, called 'The Lonesome End,' " Sheppard said. "Carpenter never went into the huddle. He just stood all alone at his end position.

"The Illini player I remember from my first game was two-way star Bill Burrell. He was from Chebanse and played guard and linebacker. He finished fourth in the Heisman Trophy voting in 1959. Halfback Billy Cannon, from Louisiana State University, won the award that year."

Burrell was recognized as the nation's top defensive player in 1959, was a two-time All-America pick and a three-time All-Big Ten selection.

"I still have the game program in my collection," Sheppard said.

Little more than three years later, on Oct. 13, 1962, Sheppard learned an important lesson about staying until the final horn sounds.

"A bunch of high school buddies and I attended the game with 10th-ranked Ohio State, and during the fourth quarter we decided to leave early," Sheppard said.

The Buckeyes held a huge lead over Illinois and the thinking was "What could possibly be of interest?"

Sheppard found out the next day.

"When I read The News-Gazette, I learned what happened," he said. "Quarterback Mike Taliaferro had thrown a 90-yard pass to Mike Yavorski for a touchdown," Sheppard said.

He heard the deafening cheers while outside the stadium, but Sheppard cannot say he saw the play that, in 2007, stands as the longest touchdown pass in Illini history.

Ohio State won the game 51-15.

Former Illinois football coach Ron Turner on the sidelines.

Rick Danz/The News-Gazette

CHAPTER 30

Sheppard was behind the microphone during the historic season of 1990, when Illinois celebrated its 100th year of football.

At halftime of one of the year's home games, several members of the 25-player All-Century Team were introduced to fans. Nearly 5,000 ballots had been cast from Illini fans throughout the country.

"Sixteen of the All-Century Team came from Illinois," Sheppard said. "California had four. Three members hailed from Indiana. Florida was represented by Mike Bass, and J.C. Caroline was from South Carolina.

"It was a great thrill for me to read off those names."

It wasn't until the 1997 season that Sheppard added the "First and 10 for the Illini" to his repertoire. It came about due to the urging of UI athletic administrator Dana Brenner.

When the Illini played at Northwestern in 1996, Sheppard and his wife, Joan, sat in the stands. They noticed Brenner with a cassette recorder on the sidelines.

"During the game, the Northwestern P.A. announcer would really pump up his voice when the Wildcats got a first down," Sheppard said. "The following week, I got a call from Brenner and we met to discuss how I could get the fans at Memorial Stadium livened up without overstepping my boundaries set by the Big Ten Conference."

For several years, Sheppard had received letters from the league office outlining the expectations for the P.A. announcer.

"One guideline stated that I needed to be impartial and not say anything directly to the fans that would cause them to cheer, such as, 'OK fans, let's cheer for the Illini,' or 'Let's make some noise for Illinois.'

"But, I could use some inflection in my voice," Sheppard said, "and so, when the Illini picked up a first down, I would say, 'First and 10 for the Illini.' I probably used the phrase a little too often when I started and some Illini fans took my intentions the wrong way.

"I said it to get our fans back in the game."

Sheppard's usage of the phrase began during a period when UI football was at one of its low points. Starting the game before the 1996 contest at Northwestern through the first 12 games Ron Turner coached at the school, Illinois lost 18 consecutive football games, ending the streak on Sept. 12, 1998, at home against Middle Tennessee State 48-20.

"Crowd noise at Memorial Stadium was at a minimum," Sheppard said.

Brenner said he realized Sheppard had to tread carefully when he added the "First and 10 for the Illini" at the appropriate time.

"The P.A. announcer's position is to give the facts basically in a non-partisan manner," Brenner said. "Not that it's stepping across the line, but it is taking it right to the edge.

"It's done in a manner that is positive. There's no negativity. It was something we could do to try and generate some enthusiasm."

Illinois and Northwestern are no longer in the minority.

"To add a little more excitement, to give it a little more home feel, a lot of schools have created something like we did," Brenner said.

Sheppard's phrase has evolved into one of his trademark expressions.

"I still use the phrase today and hopefully everyone knows why I announce it," he said.

ILLINOIS' ALL-CENTURY FOOTBALL TEAM:
(selected in 1990)

PLAYER	POSITION	HOMETOWN
Alex Agase	Guard	Evanston, Ill.
Mike Bass	Kicker	Tampa, Fla.
Dan Beaver	Kicker	Long Beach, Calif.
Chuck Bennis	Guard	Lincoln, Ill.
Al Brosky	Safety	Chicago
Dick Butkus	Linebacker/Center	Chicago
J.C. Caroline	Halfback	Columbia, S.C.
Doug Dieken	Tight end	Streator, Ill.
Tony Eason	Quarterback	Walnut Grove, Calif.
Dike Eddleman	Punter	Centralia, Ill.
Moe Gardner	Nose tackle	Indianapolis
Jeff George	Quarterback	Indianapolis
Jim Grabowski	Fullback	Chicago
Red Grange	Halfback	Wheaton, Ill.
George Halas	End	Chicago
Burt Ingwersen	Tackle	Fulton, Ill.
Jim Juriga	Guard	Wheaton, Ill.
John Karras	Halfback	Argo, Ill.
Ray Nitschke	Fullback/Linebacker	Chicago
Ed O'Bradovich	End /Punter	Hillside, Ill.
Scott Studwell	Linebacker	Evansville, Ind.
Don Thorp	Defensive tackle	Arlington Heights, Ill.
David Williams	Wide receiver	Los Angeles
Dave Wilson	Quarterback	Anaheim, Calif.
Buddy Young	Running back	Chicago

Jim and his wife Joan pose for a picture on November 20, 1999, stepson Brian Scott's Senior Day. Illinois beat Northwestern 29-7.

Jim's stepdaugter, Melissa Calkins, and her husband Will in Colorado.

CHAPTER 31

Longtime fans consider Sheppard part of the Illini family.

Though he was devoted to his duties, he's even more devoted to his own family. Sheppard's wife, Joan, is an Urbana native and a long-time teacher and dean in the Urbana Unit 116 School District.

Stepdaughter Melissa Calkins and her husband Will live in Longmont, Colo. Melissa is a UI graduate and a first-grade teacher in a Hispanic school.

Stepson Brian Scott and his wife, Stacey, have three sons: twins Camrin and Caden, and Charlie. Brian, who was inducted into the Urbana High School Sports Hall of Fame, is also a UI grad and an Illinois State police officer.

"I'm blessed with a wonderful family and very proud of each of them," Sheppard said. "The grandsons are the joy of my life."

Area sports fans never knew where they might be able to hear

Sheppard announcing if the Illini weren't at home.

"While my wife was a dean of students, I was asked to do some Urbana games, football, boys' and girls' basketball," Sheppard said. "For many years, I did high school play-by-play, so going back to do some Urbana games was enjoyable.

"I witnessed a lot of outstanding prep players, running back Morris Virgil, who later played at Illinois, J Leman, now an All-American linebacker for the Illini (and a Champaign Central graduate), and LaToya Bond, who starred for the Missouri women's basketball team before getting a shot in the WNBA.

"Doing the games at Urbana was a refreshing diversion from UI games."

Sheppard has also announced the NJCAA men's Division II basketball tournament championship game at Danville Area Community College. Even when the Illini were headed to the Final Four in 2004-05, he honored his commitment.

If there were any doubts what Sheppard would choose, they were alleviated 90 minutes prior to tipoff when he arrived at Mary Miller Gymnasium.

"Jim's most appreciated effort was when he passed on the opportunity to go with the Illini for the regional championship game in Chicago," said Mike Hulvey, the current WDAN general manager. "Jim was true to his word and came to Danville that night.

"We had assigned longtime tournament volunteer Harry Eisenhauer to keep Jim updated throughout the game so he could make the announcements to the crowd."

Eisenhauer was positioned directly behind the scorer's table with a headset tuned in to the Illini radio broadcast.

The idea worked in theory, Hulvey said.

"As the game went along, Harry got so worked up over how things were progressing with the Illini he would report the wrong score or the wrong time or keep walking in and out of the gym as he listened to the game on WDAN," Hulvey said.

"By the time the Illini made their big comeback, we got Harry settled down long enough for Jim to report the score to the crowd to a thunderous ovation."

Hulvey and Eisenhauer made certain Sheppard received something for his dedication.

"To make up for the fact that Jim missed the game in person, Harry presented to a friend of Jim's a videotape of the game at the annual WDAN Radio sports banquet so Shep could finally enjoy one of the greatest wins in Illinois basketball history," Hulvey said.

Sheppard has also done P.A. work for his alma mater, Fisher High School, as well as for Champaign Judah Christian and youth basketball in Rantoul. He filled in for Carol Wade once at a home UI women's basketball game.

"I always enjoy doing those games," Sheppard said, "and yes, people are somewhat surprised to see me at those other venues."

Sheppard's willingness to go above and beyond the call of duty is one trait that Bruce Weber finds endearing.

"He has played a huge role in organizing and running our end-of-the-year banquet, which is one of the longest running and most successful college basketball banquets in the country," Weber said. "He has also been involved with the Coaches vs. Cancer organization and helping many programs in the community be successful.

"Jim deserves a lot of credit for the work he has done and how active he has been in the Champaign-Urbana community."

Sheppard's advice to aspiring broadcasters or those interested in P.A. work is simple.

"Take advantage of as many public speaking opportunities as you can," he said. "Be willing to dedicate yourself to polishing your own skills.

"Be your own announcer; don't follow others. Know your voice and its limits. Always be prepared and double-check the information you're working with."

The joys of Jim's life: grandsons, from left, Camrin, Charlie and Caden.

CHAPTER 32

Mike Hulvey discovered how meticulous Sheppard is as he helped him in his preparations for the NJCAA championship games.

"Jim is known for being very precise in his work as an announcer," Hulvey said. "Every year, I send him the final four teams' rosters on Thursday night.

"On Saturday morning, Jim will prepare his sheets for the two teams that will play that night."

He and his wife, Joan, will make their way to the gym about 90 minutes before the scheduled start. He will meet the coaches, ask for the starters and pronunciations of each player.

"Jim will then write the phonetic spelling of each player, other than Smith and Jones, on his sheet," Hulvey said. "The DACC staff will hand Jim his script for the pregame activities, he will wait for a cue from radio announcer/Danville mayor Scott Eisenhauer, get a tap on the shoulder from me and then ..."Good evening, I'm Jim Sheppard ... ."

Once DACC received its first bid to serve as tournament host, Hulvey said, "the steering committee wanted to ensure that we presented a tournament equal to any national event."

Tournament director Dick Shockey, Scott Eisenhauer and Hulvey decided that asking Sheppard to serve as public address announcer for the finals "would be ideal."

Except for one year when Sheppard accompanied an Urbana High School delegation to Rome, he has been a fixture at DACC the third weekend in March.

"We wanted the players, coaches, fans and officials to feel like they were truly at a national championship game," Hulvey said. "If they were to hear the booming, rich sound of Jim Sheppard's voice on the P.A., there would be little doubt that something special was about to happen."

Hulvey said the feedback from fans in the stands has been positive.

"Some of the comments I've heard are, 'Wow. I was shocked to hear the Voice of the Illini in Danville,' and, 'When I heard his voice, it felt like we were at the Assembly Hall, not at Mary Miller Gymnasium,' and 'How did you get him?' "

The NJCAA tournament is put on by volunteers, and Hulvey said Sheppard fit right in despite his high-profile status.

"Shep has volunteered his time for all of his work at the NJCAA," Hulvey said. "That says a lot about him."

Brian Barnhart, the sports announcer for WDWS, learned that he and Sheppard were both sticklers for details. They often studied pronunciations together prior to games.

"We'd compare notes before games and get the proper way to say the names," Barnhart said. "He and I are a lot alike in that way. We wanted to make sure we did our homework and were on the same page.

"Jim wanted to make sure he was right. He didn't go into it in a haphazard way."

Sheppard's former colleague at WDAN, Bob Appuhn, remembers the typical reaction when a new media guide would arrive at the station.

"He'll get a look on his face and start leafing through it like a teenager with a new Playboy," Appuhn said. "Big Ten media day was like Christmas for him."

At those Big Ten gatherings, each conference school would distribute its media guides to the assembled journalists.

Though it was not a requirement for his P.A. position at Illinois, Sheppard routinely attended the weekly media luncheons.

"He was not a guy who showed up and did the games and left," Barnhart said. "He was a part of those of us who covered the games. He wanted to get the information when it was handed out (at the luncheons) and get a feel for what the coaches were saying."

From left, Dee Brown, Brian Barnhart, Jim and Deron Williams pose for a picture at the Jerrance Howard/Brian Cook basketball camp in Champaign in 2006.

Jim with the only surviving Whiz Kid, Gene Vance, in 2005.

CHAPTER 33

His birth certificate shows he's James Edward Sheppard, but those who know him well would swear his middle name is "trivia."

Sheppard has a bountiful supply of UI-related facts and figures, including some that are obscure.

"As long as I can remember, I've enjoyed the history of Illini sports and Major League Baseball," Sheppard said. "Knowledge of those two led to my interest in trivia.

"I love to toss questions and answers back and forth with friends who enjoy the same."

Jim at eight months old.

To the question, "What basketball uniform number has been the most worn at Illinois since 1940?" Sheppard said the answer is 33.

In chronological order, the list includes:

Charles Fowler	1942	Otho Tucker	1973, '75-76
Bill Erickson	1947-48, '50	Eddie Johnson	1978-81
Clive Follmer	1951-53	Ken Norman	1985-87
Harv Schmidt	1955-57	Kenny Battle	1988-89
Alan Gosnell	1958-60	Marc Davidson	1992-93
Bogie Redmon	1963-65	Kevin Turner	1995-98
Rich Jones	1966-67	Damir Krupalija	1999-2002
Jodie Harrison	1968-69	Rich McBride	2004-07
Alvin O'Neal	1971		

The second most-used numbers (with 14 apiece) by the Illini are 10 and 25.

The first to wear No. 10 since 1940 was Jake Staab (1944-45) and the latest to wear No. 10 was Jelani Boline (1997-98).

The first to wear No. 25 was Gene Vance (1941-43 and 1946-47). The latest to wear No. 25 is current player Calvin Brock, who will be a junior when the 2007-08 season begins.

Another tidbit is which former Illini played in five Super Bowls but never played college football.

That athlete was Preston Pearson, a Freeport, Ill., native who was a starting guard on Harry Combes' last two UI basketball teams in 1966 and '67.

As a running back, Pearson appeared in the 1969 Super Bowl with Baltimore, the 1975 Super Bowl with Pittsburgh and the 1976, '78 and '79 Super Bowls with Dallas.

Also from Sheppard's collection of knowledge is this item: Who is the only Illini to be named All-America in both football and basketball?

"The answer is Chuck Carney," Sheppard said. "He is from Evanston, Ill., and was a consensus All-America end in 1920. He gained All-America honors in basketball as a forward in both 1920 and 1922.

In 1966, Carney was inducted into the College Football Hall of Fame. He died in 1984."

For Sheppard's finale, the topic returned to basketball. Who are the only three men's players to average more than 20 points per game for their careers?

Nick Weatherspoon, who played from 1971 to '73, is the leader with a 20.9 average. He had 1,481 career points.

He is followed by Dave Scholz, who played from 1967 to '69, and averaged 20.5. He had 1,459 points.

The third is Don Freeman, who played from 1964 to '66, and averaged 20.1 points per game. He had 1,449 points.

Interestingly, though the Illinois basketball program is more than 100 years old, the top three scorers played within a decade of one another and prior to the creation of the three-point shot.

All good performers face the obligatory encore, and Sheppard was up to the challenge with the toughest question of all: Who is the only person born in Memorial Stadium?

"Ben Crackel was born on Jan. 21, 1925, in a 10-room apartment in the northwest corner of Memorial Stadium," Sheppard related. "Ben's parents, Ben and Margaret, had lived in the stadium since 1923.

"The senior Crackel was the superintendent of the stadium. On the day his son was born, a huge snowstorm blanketed Champaign-Urbana. Ambulances couldn't get through the fields near Memorial Stadium to take Margaret to the hospital.

"So, Dr. Charles Moss slogged through to the Crackel apartment. Nobody had a better backyard than young Ben Crackel, an instant hit at his school. Who else had 120 yards of grass to play on or five basketball courts in the (Great West Hall)?

"After a football game in the stadium, Red Grange saw the then-expectant Margaret Crackel standing on the terrace outside the apartment. Red signed a football to "Ben Jr." and had it delivered to the mother-to-be.

"Young Ben and his parents lived in the stadium until Ben Sr. died of a heart attack in 1938. On Dec. 4, 2001, Ben Crackel Jr. passed away at the age of 76. He was a longtime employee at The News-Gazette."

The News-Gazette

Ben Crackel — the only person born in Memorial Stadium — with a scrapbook of his career at The News-Gazette.

The more they collaborated, the more Barnhart realized how much he had in common with Sheppard. It went beyond, "we were in a similar line of work," Barnhart said, referring to their backgrounds in broadcasting.

Both have Orange and Blue in their blood, but Barnhart said he met his match. "He's a big trivia buff," Barnhart said, "and we quiz each other a lot of times. He knows everything about the Illinois history and the past players.

"I grew up with it, but I couldn't remember everything he did. He is so in-depth. I could never beat him in a game like that."

The News-Gazette

Ben Crackel with some old News-Gazette pages
in his room of memorabilia in 1986-87.

Former Illini basketball players Joe Cross, left, and Sergio McClain.

Jim poses with Dana Howard, an Illini linebacker
who won the 1994 Butkus Award.

CHAPTER 34

Illini fans know the public side of Jim Sheppard through his presence at the home football and basketball games.

There is another side, a private one which does not cry out for recognition or seek a place in the spotlight. It is a side seen by the players themselves.

Joe Cross is a Carbondale, Ill., native who lettered in basketball at Illinois in 2000 and '01. Six years after his graduation, he said Sheppard has had a tremendous impact on his life.

He learned early in his UI career that Sheppard wasn't a hanger-on, someone who delighted in being associated with the athletes for the prestige it brings them.

"As athletes, we know how to distinguish people who are fake and want to be around you because you play basketball," Cross said. "He is a genuine person. He enjoys all sports, but you are more than just an athlete to him, your identity is more than in your athletic ability. He challenged us: Now that you are here, what's your next step?

"Off-court time was spent in our walk through everyday issues, how to take pride in what you do. He would always relate things we did off the court, worldly issues, to the things we do on the court and how to make the transition in life.

"The things he said, he'd say, 'Just put it in your back pocket.' This guy was teaching me what would happen when I got done (playing), for situations we would be faced with."

Cross finished his fourth year as an academic counselor at Illinois when the 2006-07 school year ended. Not all of the wisdom he shares with the athletes he works with is original.

"I spit some of the things he said back out to my athletes now," Cross said.

Jim with the only two-time winner of the Heisman Trophy, Ohio State's Archie Griffin (1974-75).

He remembers specifically seeing Sheppard after returning from the Elite Eight loss to Arizona in 2001.

"He was the first one to let us know, this isn't the end," Cross said. "He said for the seniors like myself, Sergio (McClain), Nate (Mast) and Marcus (Griffin), the things we learned on the court are going to catapult us into our careers. I took that and ran with it.

"He was a guy of integrity and was always letting you know what was right off the court."

Sheppard has found that athletes are often receptive to talking about life issues.

"I've always thought a lot of athletes have a hard time mingling with the public because the public only knows them as athletes," Sheppard said. "I'd talk to them about other things than basketball, like 'How's your family?'

"To me, they are more than players. They were people who had lives and I was concerned with how they were doing. They appreciated talking about more than their sports."

Cross, in particular, was easy to get to know.

"He was very friendly, very focused and a very pleasant young man," Sheppard said.

Jim with grandsons Camrin, left, and Caden
at Illini Football Picture Day.

CHAPTER 35

Sheppard never knows when he will receive the chance to add to his extensive collection of UI memorabilia.

One of the strangest events occurred during the 1989 football season. Illinois overpowered Utah State 41-2 in a Sept. 23 game at Memorial Stadium to improve its record to 2-1.

"Sometime over night, vandals broke into the stadium and set fire to the playing field AstroTurf and destroyed over 55 yards," Sheppard said. "The crime was not discovered until Sunday morning when cleanup personnel arrived."

Workers immediately began the process of fixing the damaged turf in the two weeks prior to the Ohio State game.

"On the Friday night before the Oct. 7 game against the Buckeyes, there was a press dinner at the top of the 21-story building at Third and John streets on campus," Sheppard said. "It was a drizzly evening and I

An aerial view of Memorial Stadium.

Jim with grandsons Camrin, left, and Caden. They were teethed on Illini sports.

remember looking out the window toward Memorial Stadium.

"The man the university hired to repaint the field was still working."

A small tent had been set up at midfield and the man was putting the finishing touches on the Chief Illiniwek symbol. The next morning, the worker stopped by the P.A. booth.

"I was interested in the specialty work he was hired to do all over the country," Sheppard said, "and the many football fields he had painted.

"I asked if he'd ever made a mistake and he mentioned a time he had repainted Michigan State's football field in East Lansing. He had mistakenly painted arrows on both sides of the 50-yard line, but did not catch the mistake until he went up to the press box to survey his work."

By then, it was too late to correct the error, and the game went on.

That UI game against Ohio State was televised nationally by ABC, and the 18th-ranked Illini won 34-14.

"I lived in Indianapolis that year and a good friend of mine, John Kesler, swam a lot at the natatorium in Indianapolis," Sheppard said. "One day, he surprised me with a good piece of AstroTurf, which I still have among my Illini memorabilia.

"The natatorium had received some undamaged AstroTurf from the University after the fire, and my friend was asked if he knew anyone who would like a small piece as a souvenir."

Farewell tour: Jim and Dan Maloney, who was the final Chief Illiniwek before the tradition was retired, talk on the set of WCIA-TV's Morning Show on Feb. 22, 2007, the day after their final UI basketball game.

CHAPTER 36

In August 2006, Sheppard was summoned to the office of UI Associate Athletic Director Dana Brenner at the Bielfeldt Athletic Administration Building. UI sports information director Kent Brown was also in attendance.

Sheppard had no advance knowledge about the reason for the meeting.

"Brenner opened the conversation by asking, 'So, how do you feel about your P.A. job?' " Sheppard said. "I was somewhat caught off-guard by his question.

"I told both that I still enjoyed the position after all the years, put a lot of preparation into my announcing and, hopefully, was still doing a good job for them."

Sheppard was told that the DIA was considering a possible change for the upcoming men's basketball season.

"No reason was given," Sheppard said. "I told Brenner and Brown that I was surprised and would certainly miss announcing the games at the Assembly Hall, but that I respected their right to make such decisions.

"I asked that they notify me in ample time if a basketball change was going to occur. They agreed. We shook hands and the meeting was over."

The cloud of uncertainty hung over Sheppard's head as the 2006 football season played out. He heard nothing more until, "I finally received an e-mail from the DIA with the schedule of home (basketball) games and I was to let them know which games I could work," Sheppard said.

He responded that he was available for all of the games, including the Dec. 9 contest at the United Center in Chicago.

"The season started," Sheppard said, "and things were going along

Jim and his mother, Lucille, in California. He says
she is the greatest mom a guy could have.

just like they had in the previous 21 seasons."

There had been no additional conversations involving Sheppard about changes. Nine games into the basketball season, however, Sheppard's world was turned upside down.

In early December, Brenner called him to his office for a follow-up meeting. Brown was on hand, as was Chris Hanna, the new marketing director. Sheppard entered the room wondering why he had been summoned.

He didn't have to wait long to learn the dreaded answer.

"I was then told that the current season would be my last," he said. "I was not given any reason for the change other than the DIA 'wanted to go in a different direction.'

"I was also told they wanted me to announce the 2007 football games and that no decision had been made about 2008 football games when Memorial Stadium's renovation was completed."

A rare picture of Jim's family together. Stepson Brian and wife Joan are in back.
Stepdaughter Melissa and Jim are in front.

Though he was shocked by the edict, Sheppard broke the silence a few seconds later.

"I asked, 'Is that it?' and Brenner said, 'Yes,' " Sheppard said, "and I said, 'I'll see you in Chicago.' "

The Illini game at the United Center against Illinois-Chicago was two days away.

Brenner said the decision to dismiss Sheppard was not an easy one.

"It was very difficult," Brenner said. "Jim is a great person and provided us with a great voice, his loyalty and dedication. He only missed a handful of games at the Assembly Hall.

"That was a decision that the DIA staff made. It was not by one person, but by a number of people involved with our events and our image."

Brenner said it was tough for him to be involved in the process.

"I consider Jim a very good friend," Brenner said. "He's a great person. His loyalty and dedication to us were outstanding and will continue to be outstanding. He is a great fan of Illinois athletics."

As for going in a different direction, Brenner said that meant, "in terms of a voice and the ability during a game to present not only the game data, but the other information that is written and provided by DIA and given out through the public address system."

Sheppard found himself in a countdown to the end of the season — he had 11 games remaining to announce — but with a desire to savor every moment.

"As each game came and went, I remember that I wanted to soak in as many last memories as possible," he said.

In Sheppard's next-to-last Illini basketball game, Illinois defeated Northwestern 48-37 in a Sunday afternoon game Feb. 18. The three UI seniors, Marcus Arnold, Warren Carter and Rich McBride, erupted after the game when they learned the following Wednesday home game against Michigan would also be the finale for Sheppard.

"We love that dude," Carter said in an interview with News-Gazette sports writer Paul Klee. "It's not going to be the same coming back to the Hall without hearing his voice. I know I'm going to come back once I graduate to watch a game or two. It's going to be different."

Carter offered a solution.

"Hopefully they can record it and just play it over. That's sad. The players love him. He will be missed."

Practically before Sheppard knew it — and definitely before he was ready — the final game arrived. It was Feb. 21, 2007, against Michigan.

"I was deeply touched when I was introduced to the crowd after the game and all the Illini players and coaches approached the scorer's table to shake my hand," Sheppard said. "After the game, several fans and Orange Krush members approached me for picture requests and gave supportive comments.

"It was a very humbling experience and 22 years of wonderful memories hit me all at once."

Sheppard also received one of his most unusual autograph requests that night.

"Two students, I guessed them to be members of the Orange Krush, came up to me and one of them raised his neck and asked, 'Can you sign my throat?' " Sheppard said.

Laughing, Sheppard asked, "Are you serious?"

He was, and Sheppard took a Sharpie and signed the throat "Jim Sheppard. Go Illini."

That night conjured up memories of another bizarre request many years earlier.

"A former student approached me carrying an old trombone,"

The Orange Krush watches a video tribute to Chief Illiniwek, who was retired after the 2006-07 basketball season.

Sheppard said. "He said, 'I was a member of the Illini pep band during the Final Four season of 1989. You were a big part of that time and I'd appreciate it if you'd sign my trombone.' "

Sheppard obliged.

His farewell game against Michigan was "extra special," Sheppard said, "because my 89-year-old mother, Lucille Kirby, my wife Joan, stepson Brian and his wife, Stacey, were able to share the experience with me."

There were a series of tributes at game's end and not all were directed to the seniors who had made their final home appearance.

"My announcing work was acknowledged after the game with an announcement, followed by a long ovation," Sheppard said. "The most touching moment for me came when the Illini players and coaching staff came to me at the scorer's table and shook my hand.

"Former Illini great Kenny Battle came up, as did a lot of fans. It made it all worthwhile."

Sheppard also will cherish the salute he received from the Orange Krush.

In the waning moments of the game, members chanted, "Thank you, Sheppard."

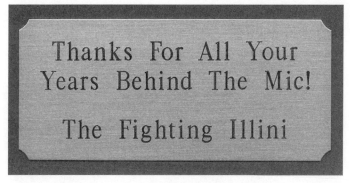

Thanks For All Your
Years Behind The Mic!

The Fighting Illini

The inscription on a plaque presented to Jim by coach Bruce Weber at the 2007 Illinois men's basketball banquet. The banquet is annually sponsored by the C-U Kiwanis Club.

The man on the right was born Saturnino Orestes Armas Minoso Arrieta on Nov. 29, 1922. He is former White Sox great Minnie Minoso.

Jim visits with ABC television announcers Keith Jackson, left, and NFL Hall of Famer Bob Griese in the Memorial Stadium press box before an Illini game.

CHAPTER 37

The reaction to the news that Sheppard would no longer be a part of the UI game day production in basketball was swift. One letter to the editor appeared in The News-Gazette the same day it was announced that Sheppard would not be asked to return following the 2006-07 season.

Those who wrote expressed feelings of support for the veteran announcer.

The first writer was Champaign's Josh May. His letter appeared in the Jan. 3, 2007, editions under the headline "Sad to hear that Sheppard is leaving."

May wrote: "I would like to express my sincere disappointment at the news that Jim Sheppard will not be returning as the public address announcer for University of Illinois basketball after this season.

"As a 22-year announcer for the UI, Jim has been such a competent and precise voice to represent our program. It is truly unfortunate that Jim's services are not being renewed, especially since it is obvious that he enjoyed the position for more than two decades.

"Jim Sheppard is an icon to his listeners, and it is sad to lose such a familiar voice that we can identify as one of our own in this community."

Three days later, another letter was printed on The News-Gazette editorial page. The writer was Josh McNattin, also from Champaign. His words were under the headline, "Sheppard belongs as UI sports announcer."

McNattin wrote: "I am shocked at the announcement that the University of Illinois Division of Intercollegiate Athletics is telling Jim Sheppard that his services are no longer required as the public address announcer for University of Illinois basketball and most likely football games.

"Since I was a kid, Jim's rich memorable voice has been an integral part of the live game experience for me. To say that he's not necessary is almost like saying we'd be just as well off printing purple and gold jerseys for the team to wear next year.

"I understand that he will have to retire someday, but so long as he is willing and able, I think he belongs in the announcer's box. I'd like to know who's taking petitions to keep him there."

A third letter of support appeared in the newspaper on Jan. 10, 2007, and was authored by Scott Horsch from Somonauk. The headline was, "Professionalism of Sheppard will be lost."

Horsch wrote: "As a University of Illinois graduate and supporter of the Illinois athletic programs, I was disappointed to learn of the dismissal of Illinois public address announcer Jim Sheppard.

"He has been a competent and dedicated professional for many years. Through this position and outside the athletic setting, he promoted the University of Illinois in a positive and passionate manner. Having had the opportunity to attend many athletic events at Illinois and other venues, I appreciate the professionalism and quality preparation that he brought to the position.

"Many public address announcers are overbearing and hard to listen to. Jim Sheppard was a recognizable and steady voice who was enjoyable to listen to.

"The changes made will result in a significant loss for the university and for the athletic program. You can certainly replace the individual, but you cannot replace the professionalism, the passion and the voice recognition that he has provided for many years at Illinois basketball and football events."

Sheppard said he was deeply touched to learn that he had such ardent supporters.

Jim says Illinois basketball has, without a doubt, the best student cheering section anywhere. These students were lining the floor for Chief Illiniwek's last performance on Feb. 21, 2007.

Darrell Hoemann/The News-Gazette

ARE YOU READY?

Jim with good friend Mike Pearson, left, Assistant Athletic Director
for Communications and Technology at Miami of Ohio.
Mike is a former Sports Information Director at the University of Illinois.

CHAPTER 38

Sheppard did not receive the chance to correct any faults his superiors might have seen.

"In the past, I had mentioned to the DIA that I welcomed constructive criticism if my style and/or comments bothered the administration, coaches, fans, players or Illini supporters," Sheppard said. "My goal was to do the best possible job."

He had not been given a list of areas that needed improvement.

"Was I angry for the change?" he asked. "Not mad, but I felt I deserved at least a candid explanation as to why, other than they 'wanted to go in a different direction.'

"When you do something for as long as I did, and embrace the position with all that you have, it becomes a part of you," Sheppard continued. "Now, I'm thankful for all the terrific Illini memories, the wonderful friendships I've made and the opportunity I was given in 1985.

"I've always been appreciative and honored to have the position."

Mike Pearson, the former UI administrator who supervised Sheppard for years, said ultimately, change is inevitable.

"That's what life is about. There are changes here and there," Pearson said. "I'm sad to see it come to an end, but Jim had a wonderful run and made his mark."

Pearson said he will remember Sheppard more for his generous nature than for being the voice behind the microphone.

"When my wife and I were moving, we had to be out of our apartment but the house we were going to was not ready to be vacated," Pearson said. "Jim and his wife invited us to stay in their home, at least for a week and maybe longer. That's the kind of guy he is, very caring and very gracious."

Sheppard will take a different view of University of Illinois basketball when the 2007-08 season opens in November. He'll return to the role he enjoyed as a child: a fan in the stands.

It won't be easy.

"I know as the next basketball season gets closer, I'll have an adjustment to make," Sheppard said. "Because my wife, Joan, has good B section seats at the Assembly Hall, I'll probably go to a few games."

He might not be the typical spectator, however. Sheppard has been conditioned to not cheer and scream and act fanatical. It's part of the age-old adage ingrained in all budding sports journalists: No cheering in the press box.

"I've never had a problem controlling my excitement when announcing," Sheppard said, "so when I attend games, my emotions will be under control. After 22 seasons of sitting courtside during many close and tense games, I simply don't overreact."

Still, there will be regrets that his time behind the microphone ended sooner than he would have hoped.

"In a lot of respects, I have lived out a childhood dream, and I know there are numerous announcers and Illini fans who envy me for what I've had the chance to do," Sheppard said. "I just wish basketball could have gone longer."

Except for continuing with Illinois football, Sheppard has no firm announcing plans. That doesn't mean he won't be heard from again.

"There is nothing planned," he said, "but I would definitely be open to considering other options."

Because a lot of Sheppard's non-working time has been devoted to UI athletics, he said, "I don't watch a lot of sports on TV.

"During the season, I do enjoy watching college football and basketball, but I can't remember the last time I watched a complete NFL regular season game. I seldom watch the NBA unless a former Illini is playing.

"I could get involved with TV sports a lot more than I do, but many other activities get my attention also."

He said the glut of games on television makes it impossible to "keep track of all who do the games."

However, Sheppard has a handful of sports commentators whom he enjoys immensely.

"Some of my favorites include Dick Enberg, Jim Nance, Steve Lavin and Bill Raftery," he said.

Champaign Central High School Hall-of-Fame coaches Tommy Stewart, left, and Lee Cabutti, right. Jim covered Stewart's football teams and Cabutti's basketball teams for years during his radio days.

CHAPTER 39

Sheppard's release from the UI basketball P.A. announcer position was one of several controversies that marked the 2006-07 school year on the Champaign-Urbana campus.

The school's cherished symbol, Chief Illiniwek, was ceremoniously retired following the same Michigan game that concluded Sheppard's career at the Assembly Hall, as well as that of the three seniors: Marcus Arnold, Warren Carter and Rich McBride.

"Even though I'm in the vast majority that wanted the Chief to stay," Sheppard said, "I really became tired of the long controversy.

"With that being said, I was still down and melancholy when the decision was made."

In a book about the history of Chief Illiniwek, Sheppard wrote, "My memories of the Chief over the past 22 years have been a little different than most fans. My view of the honored symbol has come from

Jim at the 1996 Heisman Trophy Dinner with former winner Doak Walker.
Walker played at Southern Methodist University and was the 1948 winner.

Jim with Notre Dame's first Heisman Trophy winner Angelo Bertelli
at the 1996 Heisman dinner. Bertelli was the 1943 winner.

the Memorial Stadium press box and from courtside at the Assembly Hall.

"Even though the physical presence of the Chief is gone, I will always remember what he stood for. To me, the spirit of Chief Illiniwek will never die."

There remains discussion about creating a new facility for UI home games and possibly leaving the Assembly Hall, which has been the home site for nearly five decades.

"If it was financially feasible, created better seating for all fans and enhanced our image and recruiting, I would definitely be in favor of a new basketball home for the Illini," Sheppard said. "A major question is how would the Assembly Hall survive? It's a very complex issue."

The conclusion of the 2006-07 season was bittersweet for Sheppard. Though he was not retained as the Illini P.A. announcer for home games, he was honored with the highest basketball pinnacle an individual can reach in the state of Illinois.

On April 28, 2007, in Normal, Sheppard was part of the 35th class to be inducted into the Illinois Basketball Coaches Association Hall of Fame. He had been anticipating the ceremony for months.

"I was made aware that I was being nominated when fellow Kiwanian Tom Jones (a former sports broadcaster at WCIA television in Champaign) told me that Lee Cabutti (Champaign Central's Hall of Fame basketball coach) had wanted me to send him my bio information," Sheppard said.

In December 2006, Sheppard was notified by IBCA executive director Chuck Rolinski, that he had been selected for enshrinement. Sheppard entered as a media member.

"Why did Cabutti and Jones nominate me?" Sheppard asked. "My guess is that I've announced sports for 36 years (the first 14 doing play-by-play for radio stations) and, hopefully, they thought I did it well.

Illinois basketball public address announcer Jim Sheppard
waves to the crowd as he is recognized after his last game
at the Assembly Hall in Champaign on Feb. 21, 2007.
Illinois beat Michigan 54-42.

"For several seasons in the 1960s and '70s, I announced Cabutti's games while working at WDWS. I was very honored to be chosen to this prestigious Hall of Fame. What made the event special to me was that I got to share it with my family and close friends."

Sheppard's basketball tenure might have ended, but his legacy in the sport will endure forever.

Trent Meacham, a 2007 Illini basketball player, spoke for many of his contemporaries when he said, "I want to thank him for everything he's done for the University and the athletic department over the years. I just want to wish him well."

Fred Kroner and Jim Sheppard.

ABOUT THE AUTHOR

Fred Kroner is a Mahomet native who earned his bachelor's degree in communications from the University of Illinois.

His entire sports writing career has been spent at central Illinois newspapers, starting with a part-time position at the now-defunct Champaign-Urbana Morning Courier, followed by an internship at the Springfield State-Journal Register and then his first full-time position with the Bloomington Daily Pantagraph.

In 1981, Kroner returned to his hometown and joined The News-Gazette. At one time or another, he has written about every sport that the newspaper covers, and for 17 years has handled the paper's All-State selections in girls' volleyball and basketball as well as the selections for numerous All-Area teams.

Earlier this decade, he was named The News-Gazette's Prep Sports Coordinator. In addition to covering high school events, Kroner writes a weekly column during the school year.

In 2001, Kroner was selected as the Illinois Sports Writer of the Year, an award voted on by his contemporaries and presented by the National Sportswriters and Sportscasters Association (NSSA).

He is married to the former Emily Moon, his high school sweetheart whom he often refers to as his "dream girl." He has one son, Devin Kroner, and three stepchildren, Salim Belahi, Jamel Belahi and Malika Belahi.

The Jim Sheppard book is the second authored by Kroner. In 2001, he wrote "Citizen Pain," the Brian Cardinal story.

Kroner's worst trait, according to some associates, is that he's a Cubs fan.